LOST
SUNDAYS

LOST SUNDAYS

A Season in the Life
of Pittsburgh
and the Steelers

SAM TOPEROFF

RANDOM HOUSE
NEW YORK

Library of Congress Cataloging-in-Publication Data

Toperoff, Sam.
Lost Sundays : a season in the life of Pittsburgh and the Steelers
/ by Sam Toperoff.
p. cm.
ISBN 0-394-57468-0
1. Pittsburgh Steelers (Football team)—History. I. Title.
GV956.P57T66 1989
796.332′64′0974886—dc20   89-42909

Manufactured in the United States of America
24689753
First Edition

For Art Rooney, the Chief, the philosophic gambler,
whose life was his wisest, most generous wager.

ACKNOWLEDGMENTS

I came to Pittsburgh to write about a town and its team with a vague sense that here was a place I could feel really comfortable. My many months in the city and Sundays at the stadium proved my original notion an underestimation: Pittsburgh became for me a small paradise regained.

It took awhile for this outlander—New Yorker born and bred—to be welcomed, a reluctance very typical of Pittsburghers, and which struck me as perfectly appropriate. When acceptance came, however, it was unstinting.

The media "Flies" were always helpful, especially in matters concerning the old Steelers, teams by which many of these men have measured their youths. Vic Ketchman of the *Standard Observer* and Ed Bouchette of the *Post-Gazette* led me through a good deal of unfamiliar football country. Each proofed earlier manuscripts and caught errors that might have slipped past the general public but would never have escaped true Steelers fans.

The Steelers organization is among the most open and accessible in professional sports. Art Rooney, the Chief, wanted it that way, and his son Dan has remained faithful to that ideal. Everyone connected with the team gave me the time and aid I needed. Particularly obliging were publicity director Dan Edwards and Pat Hanlon, his assistant. Joe Gordon, the team's business manager, with whom long talks about football segued into worlds beyond, became a friend. The players and coaches remained very cooperative, especially given the pressures they were under and the disappointments of the season.

I'm particularly grateful to David Rosenthal, my editor, who is a "yes" sayer, for believing there really is such a thing as a Pittsburgh mystique. And to Amy Edelman, my copy editor, whose care is unmatched in my publishing experience (would that the Steelers could draft players with her intelligence and precision). Of course, thanks to Faith and Lily for tolerating my being away *and* my not being away, and for reading my manuscripts.

Finally, to Myron Cope, who writes like Liebling and speaks like no one else on planet Earth, for his forbearance and, most important, for dubbing me a "Pittsburgh guy."

CONTENTS

LOST
SUNDAYS

1

IF THE TROPHIES
COULD ONLY TALK

It is dark in the Pittsburgh Steelers' offices. That's because they're in the bowels of Three Rivers Stadium, not higher up near the restaurant or club rooms, where they might be touched by natural light. Or where lots of NFL teams have them, miles away from the stadium on an upper floor of some glass tower amidst the downtown skyline, where they'd be indistinguishable from a law firm.

It is a special kind of dark, though, classy and slightly intimidating, a mood-setting dark rather than mere gloom—the atmosphere of a medieval castle turned into a modern museum. The decorator knew what he was after: something vaguely mysterious and fearsome, like the dynastic Steelers teams of the 1970s. He chose rich earth tones of buff and tan, burnt sienna and ocher, accented by silver gray, all highlighted with stark black and gold, the team's colors. It's likely that even if the offices were atop one of the great buildings in Pittsburgh's "golden triangle" just across the river, the Steelers would have gone for the same decor, with lots of curtains, of course.

The centerpiece—call it the altar—is in the darkest area, the spacious foyer where a visitor enters from the stadium parking lot. Baby spots illuminate a large glass case that holds the organization's icons: four silver footballs on silver pedestals, Super Bowl trophies, bearing the name of Vince Lombardi, from the seasons 1974, 1975, 1978, 1979. Until the 49ers won in 1988, only the Raiders, in Oakland and L.A., had won more than two Super Bowls ('76, '80, and '83); no team has won back-to-back since the Steelers.

No one—not players, not coaches, not Steelers office personnel, not visitors—can pass through that large, dark, low-ceilinged lobby and not notice the dramatically lighted altar in football's Church of the Last Dynasty.

During the Steelers' 1988 season, I sat unobserved for long periods of time in that lobby and watched the range of reactions of people passing the trophy case. Most of the secretaries could walk right by the altar and not even take an absent glance. The same was true for some of their bosses, especially those who had been there so long that only the absence of the trophy case would get their attention. Old-time Steelers beat writers coming in for coach Chuck Noll's regular Monday press conference could walk within a yard of the holy relics and not cast an eye. Familiarity seemed to have bred a touch of indifference.

Rarely was that the case with the players and coaches. "Mean" Joe Greene of Hall-of-Fame and Coke-commercial renown was as responsible as any man for putting the trophies there. Yet even now, after sixteen years with the organization, the last two as defensive line coach, he would amble past after a long day reviewing film and turn his head toward the shrine. Every single time.

Tunch Ilkin, the excellent offensive tackle, and Bryan Hinkle, the outside linebacker, eight- and seven-year veterans respectively at the start of the '88 season, always looked at the trophies as they passed. So did Tony Dungy, the defensive coordinator, who earned a Super Bowl ring as a defensive back on the '78 team.

Virtually everyone directly associated with these on-field Steelers looked at the trophies every time. Poor won-lost records in recent years had created an even deeper personal awareness of the sacrifice, determination, pride, and of course *talent* that won those silver footballs. They represent what it takes to be excellent.

As the 1988 season unfolded, reactions to the Super Bowl trophy case told the story of the Steelers more explicitly than any football analysis. After Sunday home games, for example, the families and friends of the players crowded the dim lobby waiting for husbands and fathers and heroes to get dressed, deal with the press, and trudge from the locker room. After the first game, one mother warned her curious, active boy, "Don't be touching that glass, Reggie." Reggie was not alone in his fascination.

By midseason, with the team at 2-6, the crowd in the lobby after games was not only subdued, it had backed away from the trophy case as though it were contaminated. The team's performance had deteriorated terribly, and it was too painful for the families and friends of proud men to confront those symbols of unmatched excellence. The trophies seemed to be judging the players and to have found them wanting.

By season's end, the record was still woeful. Statistically, the defense was the poorest in the entire league, and the offense wasn't a great deal better. Many players felt extremely uncomfortable walking past the trophy case; a few even preferred to leave by another, more distant door.

If those trophies could have talked during the season, they would have spoken forthrightly to the players. In September they would have said, "We are what you must aspire to. We are what is expected of you. You must deliver, if not this season, then the next. This season, though, you must give some sign of worthiness. You must accept our challenge." And they would have begun to chant names: "Greene. Harris. Bradshaw. Greenwood. Ham. Lambert. Blount. Swann. Bleier . . ."

At season's end, they seemed to say: "You haven't done at all well.

You did not honor us. No, you were not at all worthy. So hear more of the names: Russell. Stallworth. Shell. Holmes. Wagner. Webster. Mansfield. Edwards. White . . ."

Father Myles Kavanaugh, a priest from the Olde Sod and a longtime intimate of the Rooney family, which has been the sole owner of the Steelers franchise for half a decade, heard the trophies muttering late in the year and suggested to Dan Rooney, the team president, that it might be time to consider removing the altar. Presenting young players with a standard they're unable to meet, he argued, can be too much of a challenge. It can dishearten them and break their spirits. Why not just lower the expectations for a while? Remove the trophies, Dan, me boy-o.

But, the counterargument runs, the old Steelers dynasty *did* exist; it was real men winning real football games with remarkable efforts. Their accomplishments should be writ large to be read by all throughout the ages, not dismissed with a trick of revisionist history. At least nine and as many as eleven of the men who played on those teams are destined for the Football Hall of Fame. True excellence is true excellence—let's not kid ourselves or the young players coming along about that. And, damn it, let's not be dishonest about what it takes to get to the top and stay there in this exacting world. If some of these players can't cut it, then cut some of these players and find ones who can. Don't remove that trophy case.

The stunning failure of the '88 team, coming after five years of general mediocrity, forced Rooney, Noll, and the entire organization into a series of very difficult choices. The gut-wrenching decisions these men were going to have to make would cost players and coaches and front-office men their jobs. The basic philosophy behind all the choices, though, would be symbolized by one nonfootball question: Would the Super Bowl trophies stay in the lobby for everyone to have to confront?

Dan Rooney wanted to think for a long while about that one.

*

The season was not supposed to have been a disaster, though it didn't figure to be a Super Bowl year either. Informed and reasonable hopes were for meeting some of the team's glaring needs with young players and thereby ending the season a game or two over .500. No less an expert than *Sports Illustrated*'s "Dr. Z," Paul Zimmerman, whose preseason picks are often uncannily accurate, had the '88 Steelers at 9-7, second in the AFC Central behind Cleveland, yet good enough to make the playoffs as a wild card.

There seemed to be enough young talent to accomplish that. Then there was always the chance of getting some lucky bounces in crucial games and ending up 10-6, or even better, and winning the division outright. Many stranger things had happened.

Even though he is anything but a wishful thinker, Noll had said, "Once a team makes the playoffs, anything can happen. Just win two or three games and you're in the Super Bowl." And by extension, just get a little lucky in the Super Bowl, and you win it all. Trophy number five. In Pittsburgh it's known as "one for the thumb," a phrase Mean Joe Greene coined because he had Super Bowl rings on all his fingers but the last.

It's all true enough, but not quite true either. Teams that go to the Super Bowl are never lucky football teams. They're very good football teams that have a bit of luck along the way.

Since their last Super Bowl appearance in January 1980, the Steelers have been a model of NFL "parity" (Commissioner Pete Rozelle's euphemism for inferiority), winning—or losing, if you prefer—roughly half the time. To Pittsburghers spoiled by a dynasty, *parity* is another word for creeping failure, roughly akin to saying America has attained parity with Japan and Germany.

The Steelers' brain trust intended 1988 to be the first sure, measurable step in the direction of the NFL's upper echelon. It wouldn't be a complete make-over of the 1987 team; that wasn't deemed necessary. This was already a very young team, one of the youngest in the league, but the fabric had some holes in important places, and the intention at training camp was to discover and develop players who could fill those holes and make them positions of strength in the years to come.

In strike-marred 1987, the Steelers had an 8-7 record and lost a chance at a playoff position on the last week of the season by losing at home to Cleveland by six points. The season was so skewed by general squad instability, postponements, and strike games that any conclusions based on that season's performances were tenuous at best. Still, it was all anyone had to go by.

Defense is the key element on a Chuck Noll team. He subscribes to the NFL truism *Offense wins games; defense wins championships.* Smart organizations usually start building with defense; they know a good one can keep them in ball games regardless of how ineffective their offense may be. Staying close always gives you a chance to win. In addition, drafting for defense is more predictable than drafting for offense. At bottom, defense requires will and controlled rage, offense a variety of athletic skills that may or may not translate to the NFL from the college game. If a team relies on the passing game, for example, finding young players with the combination of skill, strength, speed, and adaptability professional football requires is difficult. Drafting them is chancy. Furthermore, in the Steelers' particular case, because they play so many of their games in the league's northern cities, where the offense has the additional problem of coping with harsh weather conditions, Noll has always stressed defense.

One reason the Steelers were picked to do fairly well in 1988 was their steadily improving defense. Their '87 draft focused on shoring up the secondary and linebacking corps: Five of their first seven selections were players projected for those positions. All of them made the team: Cornerback Beltin' Delton Hall, so named because he hurt people and seemed to like it, was named to a number of All-Rookie teams at season's end. At the other corner, Rod Woodson, the world-class hurdler from Purdue, held out until October and didn't get as much playing time, but everyone knew he was a "player." Free safety Thomas Everett was Napoleonic—small and always trying to prove something to the world by being an oversized hitter.

The Steelers' long tradition of excellent linebacking seemed secure. The popular outside linebacker Mike Merriweather was voted the team's Most Valuable Player. Outside backer Bryan Hinkle had won the award the year before and, though playing hurt much of the time, made a real contribution. David Little, who replaced the incomparable Jack Lambert when he retired in 1984, led the team in tackles. The veteran Robin Cole, a former Pro-Bowler, played well enough, but much to the coaching staff's delight, he was being pushed for playing time by Hardy Nickerson, a rookie.

The team's major defensive problem was in the line, where hardly any of the draft choices of recent years ever seemed to play up to expectations. Because the Steelers needed down linemen badly, desperately in fact, their first choice in the April 1988 draft was Aaron Jones, a pass rusher from Eastern Kentucky University. It was a choice utterly unexpected by most football people.

The draft was televised on ESPN, the sports cable network. When the Steelers selected Jones, Chris Berman, the announcer said, "Hmmm . . . a player projected further down . . . a pass rusher . . . the Steelers apparently think—"

Sitting alongside him, *S.I.*'s Paul Zimmerman interrupted Berman's tap dance: "Let's face it, we're all shocked."

At twenty-one, one of the youngest players in the National Football League, Aaron Jones was a very long shot to meet the team's most obvious need. Early in training camp a reporter asked Aaron how many sacks he expected to have in his rookie season. Aaron thought a minute and drawled, "I'd say between eighteen and twenty would sound about right." Quite a daring prophecy, to put it mildly, since Aaron had only nine sacks his senior year at Eastern Kentucky University. Just for comparison's sake, over a thirteen-year career Mean Joe Greene had sixty-six.

Yes, Aaron Jones was refreshing, but could he play? Only time would tell. A first-rate pass rusher had been a priority for the Steelers ever since the famed Steel Curtain, consisting of Greene, L. C. Greenwood, and Dwight White, and abetted by Fats Holmes, began to unravel. Things had looked promising indeed when the Steelers took Gabe Rivera from Texas Tech in the '83 draft. In his first few games, the rookie was so impressive he won the nickname "Señor Sack," and you don't get a nickname in Pittsburgh cheaply. Rivera seemed to be the answer to the Steelers' prayers.

But other prayers would be necessary. On a wet and slippery highway in late October that same year, Rivera's Datson 280ZX slid across the median and spun into another auto. Señor Sack was thrown through the rear window of his car with such force that his spine was crushed on impact. He is now a paraplegic.

None of the legion of pass rushers the Steelers have drafted since have filled the void. It was as though the gods had decreed no more curtains of any kind ever again. Aaron Jones was simply the latest pass-rushing hope. Jones's task of breaking into the big time, however, promised to be made a little easier by the presence of the veteran Keith Willis, who, through hard work and intelligent application of technique, had become a respectable pass rusher. If Jones could deliver, the tandem would be more than twice as effective as two individuals. They'd begin to constitute a defensive threat up front.

Another major defensive cavity might be at nose tackle, where thirty-five-year-old Gary Dunn had played his heart out for eleven seasons. Dunn hadn't ever been outstanding, but he had been professional, consistent, and good against the run. His knees, however, had hobbled him from his first full season on, and he had played an entire career in pain. Dunn was a triumph of mind over cartilage, and he believed he could hold up for one more season.

Donnie Shell, the strong safety, had finally retired after fourteen seasons. His four Super Bowl rings and career interceptions total will be his entrée to the Hall of Fame, and no replacement could provide his on-field coaching or his fire. Adequacy was all Noll hoped for from the strong-safety position, and probably all he needed.

Cornerback Dwayne Woodruff was now the veteran of the unit, a nine-year man with a Pittsburgh Super Bowl ring on his finger, and expected to provide leadership for the talented youngsters back there. If the secondary could play back to the previous season's opportunistic aggression—they had led the league in interceptions run back for touchdowns—and maintain their performance one more season, two of the three defensive building blocks, backers and secondary, would be solid.

Each defensive subunit—down linemen, linebackers, and secondary—must respond immediately and instinctively to what the others are doing. It takes time to develop the "feel," one man for the other, all good defenses have. An NFL offense is supposed to operate like a perfectly balanced, well-oiled machine; a defense, however, is really a complex organism, a living whole greater than the sum of its parts when it's healthy, full of mysterious illnesses when it's not.

The organism is supposed to be cultivated during training camp, where there is the time and supervision to let that special feel among defensive players develop. The four preseason games (Rozelle didn't want them called "exhibitions") should determine if the organism is durable and if the parts can cohere enough to grow into a reliable NFL defense.

If the Steelers' defense had some weak spots, the offense had obvious holes at the most crucial places—quarterback, running back, wide receiver. Brains, legs, hands.

Mark Malone, the maligned starting quarterback for the previous four seasons, had played himself out of a job at least a year and a half earlier, but he was still at the helm at the end of '87 because there was no adequate replacement. You don't find franchise quarterbacks on waiver lists, and there were never any blue-chip college boys around when the Steelers' turn came up in recent drafts.

A heartbreaking player who could look superb one week and like a sandlot player the next—or, more exasperatingly, from one *quarter* to the next—Malone had driven fans, coaches, and teammates bananas. Because quarterback play is so visible and the Steelers looked competent and competitive at many other positions, most fans assumed Malone was the team's only problem.

Noll, who had stuck with Malone far beyond reasonable doubt, had no choice but to cut him loose after the '87 season. If he hadn't, there would certainly have been a revolt even in the ranks of the loyalists. Malone was traded to the San Diego Chargers, who the Steelers were scheduled to play late in the '88 season.

Walter Andrew Brister III, nicknamed "Bubby" by his five older sisters, had been Malone's backup since he was drafted in the third round out of Northeast Louisiana University in 1986. He started two games in his rookie year when Malone was hurt, but though he showed flashes, he simply wasn't ready. He backed up Malone in '87 and never started a game.

Because he was a colorful character from Louisiana who appeared to appreciate a good time better than an evening with his playbook, he was immediately compared to a great Steelers quarterback of similar background and inclination, Terry Bradshaw. Like Bradshaw when he first came to Pittsburgh, Brister was an exceptional athlete with a powerful arm. And also like Bradshaw, there were whispers about Bubby's lack of intelligence and commitment to excellence— whispers, by the way, that were always impossible to track back to any reliable source.

Brister didn't appear to be Noll's kind of guy. Bradshaw hadn't been either. Brister had a "bad boy's" flair, and temperamentally Chuck preferred "good boy" quarterbacks; Malone, for example, was a boy scout. Unsure that Brister could do the job, the Steelers traded a fourth-round draft choice for the Kansas City quarterback Todd Blackledge, a quintessential "good boy." Blackledge, a Phi Beta Kappa, had led Penn State to the national championship in 1982. If credentials played quarterback, his had the job over Bubby's.

Blackledge had some fine games at Kansas City, but he couldn't do the job consistently enough to satisfy the coaching staff there. The hope in Pittsburgh was that a change of scene would revive him. In a sense, Blackledge was coming home: He hailed from Canton, Ohio, and his father, Ron, was Chuck Noll's offensive-line coach.

Brister's experience couldn't compare with Blackledge's, who had started twenty-four NFL games. Nevertheless, Bubby was sure 1988 was his year. He told reporters when he arrived in training camp in July, "I'm the *man*. Write it down." In spite of his confident assertion, the job was considered open by the coaching staff when training camp began.

The key man in most NFL offenses is the quarterback, but Noll's football philosophy was based on an effective running game. And the bread and butter of the ball-control ground game was Noll's complex trap-blocking variations, in which linemen opened holes that the running back had to hit at the proper moment. The offensive line was one of the Steelers' assets, composed of men small by NFL standards but quick and smart—Noll's preference in linemen. There was experience here with Ilkin at tackle, Craig Wolfley, an eight-year veteran, at guard, and Mike Webster, the many-time All-Pro, at center.

Replacing the great trap blockers of the Super Bowl years had not been easy and could only get harder. Bill Nunn, who had scouted southern colleges for the Steelers for decades, worried more than ever about finding the kind of players who would fit Noll's needs. "It's too sophisticated a system for colleges to use these days. They're all going for giants who can hold their ground; Chuck wants these fast smaller kids with some blocking techniques. Let me tell you, they're tough to find. Guess we'll have to do what we usually do—draft the right kind of athlete and teach 'em all the techniques ourselves."

Timing and intelligence—hitting the proper hole at the proper moment—is what Noll looks for first in a running back. He hadn't had a great power runner since Franco Harris retired in '84, but the team did get to the '84 AFC championship game with Frank Pollard carrying the load.

Even when the trapping system was working well, however, an outside running threat remained a desirable option. That's precisely where a back with speed enough to fake inside, get to the corner, and turn upfield would be an enormous boost. The Steelers hadn't had a back like that for a good long while.

The receiving corps was moribund. John Stallworth, another four-time Super Bowler and certain Hall of Famer, had become a marvelous possession receiver when he slowed down in his later years. Unfortunately, Stallworth hung up his cleats at the end of the '87 season. Louis Lipps, a wonderful deep threat in his first two seasons, '84 and '85, hadn't come close to approaching that form. Lipps was so good then and so unreliable the next two seasons, some of the fans who used to yell *Loooooo* whenever he made an impossible catch, shifted to *Boooooo* when he didn't make a reasonable one.

Filling the team's other glaring holes had been such a priority for the scouting department that pass-catching help was going to be a matter of catch-as-catch-can.

A look at the ages of the players invited to the 1988 training camp revealed this was a team of two disparate categories—the very old and the very young. There wasn't much of a middle ground. For the Steelers to meet or go beyond popular expectations, a great many of the young players were going to have to show they had come of age in the NFL. Or, as Delton Hall put it, "Got to show up, stand up, put up, and deeee-liver." The place to find out who could deliver was training camp.

When the letter from the Steelers arrived in the mail for rookies and free-agent invitees, it must have been a thrilling moment, with relatives and friends soon stopping by to see Chuck Noll's scrawled signature. It began cordially enough: "This letter should be construed as your official invitation to report to the Pittsburgh Steelers Training Camp at St. Vincent College in Latrobe, Pennsylvania, Sunday, July 17, 1988, at 12:00 noon. . . ."

It ended in typical Noll fashion—"In short, an aggressive football team in all areas, peopled with aggressive players who want to have fun. FUN IS WINNING!"

In between was the scary part: "To realize our goal of being the best team in the NFL starts with being the *best conditioned team* in the NFL, the team who wins them in the fourth quarter." It was very clear, at least to the veterans who had attended other Noll camps, that pain was implied in those italics. They also knew the youth movement was on, and were keenly aware of what jobs were up for grabs and just how rough the competition would be.

I had met Art Rooney, Sr., the revered chairman of the board of the Steelers, only once. It was at the start of the miserable 6-10 1986 season, when *Sports Illustrated* sent me down to Pittsburgh to do a story on Malone, a quarterback under seige. The day I walked into the Steelers' offices at 300 Stadium Circle for the first time, I was drawn to the trophy case. Naturally. This was the earth's navel for a football fan.

An old man shuffled alongside as I was trying to read some of the inscriptions on the footballs. I should have recognized the ruddy, slightly fleshy Irish face, certainly the shock of white hair, thick glasses, and oversized cigar, from the times I'd seen Pete Rozelle handing this man a silver football on television. I didn't. In fact, I thought in some vague way he was part of the custodial staff, someone they just kept around for old times' sake.

I said, because he seemed to be waiting for me to make a comment, "Really something, aren't they?"

"Think so?" he said.

"Four in six years. Those had to be some teams. No one can ever know the effort that must have gone into winning them."

"Amen."

We waited in silence for a while. I began to get sentimental before the icons.

He took a long draw and blew cigar smoke past the trophy case. "Don't forget the luck."

Surprised, I said, "Don't you think great teams make their own luck?"

His eyes flashed behind the thick lenses. "To a certain extent. It's also what people like to believe. But what if Bradshaw or Greene or Lambert or Harris had gone down? You think they'd have won?"

I thought about it. I wasn't sure, but said, "Yes, I think they would have."

He smiled, thrust out his hand, and introduced himself. I felt as though I had passed a test.

THE SPIRIT OF PLACE

Most professional sports franchises have the local loyalties of a multinational corporation. They will move wherever the veins run deepest and the residual checks have the most zeroes. There are, however, some notable exceptions, teams and places that are so bound together by bonds of history, identity, and mystique that tearing them apart is as improbable as improbable gets. ("Impossible" is just not applicable where human greed is concerned.) Pittsburgh and its Steelers have formed such a bond, and it's a pretty intense affair.

If you want to learn about the "Stillers" (as the team is known in local dialect), talk to Pittsburghers about their city. If you want to know the city, talk about the "Stillers." You'll discover you've learned about the bond as well. Of course, what you learn depends on who you talk to. And it depends mostly on how long they've lived in Pittsburgh and how closely they've identified with the team. Chances are, if they say "Stillers," you'll learn a lot.

Ahiro Okawa does not say "Stillers"; in fact, he has trouble saying the word in any recognizable way. Mr. Okawa was not born in Pittsburgh. He was born in Nagasaki, Japan, in 1945—a year when more Japanese were dying than were being born, especially in

Nagasaki. In 1980 he moved to Sewickley, a wooded, fancy middle-class suburb west of Pittsburgh. Mr. Okawa is a representative of a Japanese industrial monolith that is producing small amounts of "specialty" steel in a Monongahela River minimill. Allegheny-Ludlum is the sole American firm operating here in the same capacity. Just about the only kind of steel still being made in Pittsburgh on a regular basis, "specialty" is produced by a handful of Pittsburgh workers. Mr. Okawa's company employs 120 men in a mill town upriver that once employed over 9,000 steelworkers.

In a sense, Mr. Okawa is the enemy here. The Japanese, most prominently but not exclusively, have subsidized their own steel industries for a long while, but they began to do so heavily in the early 1970s. The French and Germans and British and Swedes and Koreans do the same. Over the years and for a variety of reasons, the American steel giants found it harder and harder to compete, and the Rust Belt was born. Pittsburgh—Steeltown, U.S.A.—was emasculated in little more than a decade.

In Pittsburgh, a Japanese national is a lot more visible than other foreigners, and more obviously connected to a heavy manufacturing firm—electronics being the only other possibility—but Mr. Okawa stands up bravely to the occasional stares he gets. They are only occasional because where he lives and travels, he meets very few unemployed steelworkers. His neighbors are upper-echelon managers like himself, but from the service industries that arose when foreign competitors helped knock out large-scale steelmaking.

Even as steel was starting to go down for the count in the late seventies, the Steelers were unquestionably one of the best damn teams ever to kick ass on NFL turf, real or artificial. If you look at the entire decade, they were *the* best. There was, of course, something wonderful about a team named after an industry, taking for its insignia the U.S. Steel trademark, representing a hard-bitten, smoky, one-industry town. But if the Steelers were a true reflection of what was going on in the steel industry at the end of the decade, with its massive layoffs, they would have put only six men on the field. Either that, or played with eleven and called themselves the Rising Suns.

Okawa is not at all the stereotypic Japanese businessman operating in America, not the silent, unobtrusive observer, hiding behind a deadpan game face. He is tall, around six feet, and appears to have learned his English from an eccentric tutor, because he is refreshingly slangy, direct, and borderline outrageous in his conversation.

I noticed him for the first time knotting and reknotting his tie on a very public shuttle bus. "Red," Okawa said to me across the aisle, pointing to his wild paisley. "Red tie is power symbol. Said so on TV. Red is power. Crazy American idea. What the heck, I say to myself, here need all the power I can get." What made the power-tie theory even more absurd was that Okawa's tie ended just below his sternum.

Although he gets offers of free tickets to Steelers games, Okawa has gone to Three Rivers Stadium only twice, with his teenaged son. "Terrible team, terrible team. Lose both times. Both times blowout. Team so bad, embarrassing to witness. Good in seventies, everyone say. Super Bowl all the time. No more, no more. Maybe year 2000. My son will have son before Steelers good team again."

I asked Mr. Okawa if he knew how or why a team that was so incredibly good could turn mediocre and then bad so quickly.

He did, sort of. "Football like war. War like being in steel business. If successful, win, win, win, win. But lose too, sometimes. Nobody win all the time. Is matter of cycles. History, business, football, everything. Even great general, great coach like Chuck Noll, must lose to learn from losing. Noll like Japanese emperor. He learn to lose, learn he is not a god, not perfect. Maybe Steelers lose because Noll not perfect anymore, not a god. Perhaps has been emperor of Pittsburgh too long. He should be the last emperor, get it? Har-har-har."

*

Frank Krupka, Jr., is in his early forties, a Stillers season ticket holder since 1971, eyewitness to Franco Harris's "Immaculate Reception" at Three Rivers that beat the Oakland Raiders in the AFC playoff game two days before Christmas, 1972. That lucky deflection and touchdown run coincided with the Steelers' coming of age: They were becoming a very, very good football team; the luck just made the birth of their inevitable success slightly premature. Frank Krupka, Jr., was there for all the great years. "If I never have another shot at a Super Bowl, at least I've had the seventies Stillers," he'll tell you over every odd round of beer.

My meeting with Frank junior was arranged by his father, another season ticket holder. (We're going to meet Frank senior later. He's an important character in this tale of Pittsburgh.)

Frank Krupka, Jr., tells me he comes from Aliquippa, a mill town without a mill these days. Aliquippa sits along the Ohio River twenty-five miles west of Pittsburgh. But he doesn't *come* from Aliquippa, he *came* from Aliquippa. He has lived in Coraopolis, a suburban town closer to the city proper, since 1978. Frank junior and his first marriage were early victims of the first round of layoffs from the big LTV steel plant in Aliquippa. His father, who had much more seniority, hung on till the bitter end in 1983.

The younger Krupka held things together on unemployment checks and by doing small repairs on old houses. That eventually became Krup's Home Improvement Company. With success and stability came a second wife, a large house in Coraopolis, and financial security. So why does he tell me he's from Aliquippa?

Because, for the purposes of a book on the Steelers, Frank Krupka, Jr., wants to be identified with the gritty cobblestone streets and the work boots that trudged over them to and from the mill. He loved those good times as a mill-town man: an "Imp and an Iron"—a shot of Imperial whiskey and Iron City beer—with the boys in the tavern on the way home from work; shooting the bull about sex that didn't happen and football that did, but not exactly the way it was remembered; and at the heart of things, football, always football—Aliquippa High School games up on the hill Friday nights, college games on TV Saturdays, the Stillers at Three Rivers on Sunday.

Frank junior says he played linebacker his senior year at Aliquippa. In this region, that's the only credential a man needs. Aliquippa's Aschman Stadium is one of the sacred places. Mike Ditka wore the red and black of the Aliquippa "Fighting Quips." In the minds of most old-timers, Ditka plays there still. Frank junior chooses to represent Aliquippa as home. It is his spiritual place.

"Sure," he admits, "the Stillers have come on hard times, but they're gonna pass. They get a few decent draft picks, there'll be no stopping them." Doesn't Krupka see that's just about the equivalent of saying the mills will open again, the sky will glow red at night, the air quality will plummet, and Frank Krupka, Jr., will move back to Aliquippa and take a job as a mill hand? In his fantasy, he might even remarry his first wife.

When the layoffs began, a lot of other things were happening at once, all of them bad. The aftermath of Vietnam reverberated still. The civil rights movement and the murder of Dr. King left a legacy of racial antagonism for years in a city where competition for a declining number of jobs was predictably bitter. All the social disruption was intensified by economic hardship and dislocation. Very bad times in Steeltown.

"At least the Stillers are winning" is what men, fearing that steelmaking was finished in Pittsburgh, said to each other. Black players and white players, meshing well for three hours on a football field, won football games, won championships, and did it in a way that reflected how lots of Pittsburghers were feeling. Sick and tired of getting booted around, they wanted *their* team not just to win, but to take *their* pound of flesh on Sunday. At Three Rivers, that was usually what happened. No team had ever been asked to fulfill so many human needs as those Steelers.

Those needs were met remarkably: 1974, 10 wins, 3 losses, 1 tie, victory in Super Bowl IX; 1975, 12 wins, 2 losses, victory in Super Bowl X; 1976, 10 wins, 4 losses; 1977, 9 wins, 5 losses; 1978, 14 wins, 2 losses, victory in Super Bowl XIII; 1979, 12 wins, 4 losses, victory in Super Bowl XIV.

Unlike so many of the ingrate fans of Krupka's age, whose anger over the latest Steelers team is a full pendulum swing from their pleasure over the seventies Steelers, part of Frank junior remains forever grateful. "What all the Stiller players, the Rooneys, and Chuck Noll gave this town for so many years, we were lucky to get. No other town ever had anything like it. Just to have lived through it once was enough. To see Lambert and Rocky and Brad, Franco and Swann and Stallworth, Joe Greene, Mel Blount, Jack Ham, all those guys—Jesus, that was more than anyone had a right to deserve. I guess a lot of us got spoiled, thought teams like that were our due, but at least we had that. We were the pinnacle of professional football, and no one can ever take that away—ever." Krupka's voice quivers; his eyes fill.

But what of the future? Must future Pittsburghers be content with other men's memories? "No, no, we'll be back eventually. We have to be. It's common sense. Chuck came in 1969, and his first team won only one game. But he built through the draft and just five years later, the boys won their first Super Bowl. We just have to be patient."

Very few of Krupka's contemporaries are as patient and trusting of Noll and the Steelers organization. "Maybe," said a tailgater pulling on a green bottle of Rolling Rock in the parking lot after a miserable Steelers performance, "that kind of bullshit football might be tolerated in Tampa Bay or Atlanta or Kansas City. It won't be tolerated here. This is Pittsburgh." And his friends pumped fists into the crisp air and shouted, "Yeeaargh."

*

Arthur McEnery has a perspective shared by very few Steelers fans, by very few Pittsburghers. McEnery is seventy-eight. He lives in Oakland, a small city within the confines of the larger city. Civilized, decorous, home to the University of Pittsburgh and the renowned Children's Hospital—all symbolized by the university's towering Cathedral of Learning—Oakland has always been atypical of Pittsburgh. A touch of refinement among the working-class enclaves.

Arthur McEnery graduated from Pitt in 1934 with a degree in history, which he says served him no useful good when he took a temporary job in the university's business office. He stayed only fifty-one years. McEnery never married. "No room in my heart," he supposes. "My passion for football, and slightly less for baseball, consumed me. I spent my youth on the Forbes Avenue trolley and in the bleachers at Forbes Field watching the Pirates. The sporting life in Pittsburgh in those days got divided up neatly by seasons. Baseball all summer. College football in the fall. Hot-stove league in the winter. Spring training in the spring."

In 1933, Arthur Joseph Rooney brought a professional football franchise in the National Football League to Pittsburgh. It was the fifth franchise in the new league, and Mr. Rooney called his team the Pittsburgh Pirates. "I suppose he did that to create an association with the baseball team, which was already well established," McEnery says. "Art Rooney was already a well-known character around town, an excellent athlete in many sports in his youth, then a sports promoter, and always a gambler. Legend was that he bought the football franchise with twenty-five hundred dollars he won at the races in Saratoga. It's a nice romantic legend."

The football Pirates looked like a very bad bet for Art Rooney. McEnery recollects, "When I'd go out to Forbes Field to see the football Pirates play the Chicago Cardinals and the Bears, the Packers and the Giants, there were often more players in the stadium than spectators, surely more than any actual paying customers. I must admit, I slipped in myself without paying some of the time. Rooney's Pirates were dreadful."

So dreadful, in fact, that they started playing some of their "home" games in Youngstown, Ohio, as well as in Louisville and New Orleans. And they stayed dreadful even when Mr. Rooney signed Byron "Whizzer" White, the present Supreme Court Justice, in 1939 for the then largest salary in pro ball—a truly astounding Depression-era $15,800.

"Whizzer drew a few people," says McEnery, "because he was the league's leading rusher, one of its biggest stars." But he didn't help win games; they won only one his first season. They won only two games when Mr. Rooney changed the team's name to the Steelers in 1940. During World War II, to conserve manpower and fuel, the Steelers combined their roster with that of the Philadelphia Eagles in 1943 and the Chicago Cardinals the following year. Collectively they won five and lost fourteen. You might say the actual Steelers were only 2½-7. Arthur McEnery still wonders at that: "Can you imagine a team representing two cities with two head coaches? I must have had a perverse streak in those days. I always went back, even though sometimes it was hard to find where the team was playing—sometimes it was at Pitt Stadium, more often at Forbes Field.

"I'd go so far as to say," McEnery offers, "that no professional football team has ever been as bad for as long as the old Stillers and Pirates and Steagles and Stardinals were." It is a lovely touch that as well educated and devoid of the local accent as Arthur McEnery has attempted to be, he still can't help but say "Stillers."

The record supports McEnery's memory of all those teams. Wherever their home, whatever their name, they won 162 games and lost 272 in the NFL from 1933 until Chuck Noll arrived as head coach in 1969.

Arthur McEnery appreciates the Steelers in the long term. "I'm sure the experts will analyze the latest fall of the team down to the nub and come up with dozens of esoteric explanations. Well, I don't think it's a very complicated matter. I subscribe to the luck-of-the-draw theory. Chuck Noll was there when the Stillers drafted magnificent players in the seventies. He was still there when the drafts failed in the eighties. Either Noll was smart in the seventies and got extremely dumb in the eighties, or it's all a matter of the luck of the draw. Luck plays such a great part in life in general and sports in particular, that it's as good an explanation for me as any."

McEnery sees the 1988 season as a throwback to Mr. Rooney's old Pittsburgh Pirates and appreciates them for that: "I watched every game to the bitter end on TV. I'm beyond 'win or lose' now, I'm just happy to see the Stillers play. We've won more than our share of Super Bowls. It's time to give some of these other cities a chance. They've been deprived."

With Steelers history, as with history in general, there is a price to pay for ignorance. Plenty of contemporary Steelers fans, without Arthur McEnery's perspective, are paying it now. "I didn't realize," says Judith Klein, an industrial psychologist with her own consulting firm, "how important the Steelers have been to the men of Pittsburgh. I was working on a project in Johnstown after the mills there shut down in the early eighties. Things were extremely bad in town. The entire region was severely depressed. It didn't look as if the people would be able to survive. Our intention was to find among the laid-off workers those with potential entrepreneurial ability, retrain them, and start them off in small businesses. Not much, I'm sorry to say, ever came of our search. But during my interviews it hit me what the Steelers really meant to these men. One phrase kept coming up over and over again—'Things are so bad around here, even the Stillers are doing lousy.'"

The "even" was the giveaway. It meant that, when all was said

and done, their bedrock belief, their psychological underpinning—
the seventies Steelers—could crumble. *Even* they. Pittsburgh steel,
the men who produced it, and, yes, *even* the Steelers had become
irrelevant. Nothing was forever.

McEnery knew that. Anyone with a knowledge of history knew
that. Permanence was pure illusion, impermanence was life's rule.
Dynasties rose, dynasties fell. They didn't rise very often, but those
that did, fell certainly.

A psychologist could see quite clearly that these men, especially
the macho blue-collar types who were losing their personal effectiveness, had attached themselves emotionally to an intimidating
football team that was still the scourge of the league. Everyone
around the league feared the Steelers of the seventies. They were
rough, they were borderline dirty, they were effective. For these fans,
the association was psychological projection. But it was more than
that. It was myth—that is, factual history transformed into legend
and stamped with timelessness.

Though the current team is a poor one, the myth of the team that
once was shines through in spite of everything. You hear it whenever
men get together to drink beer and talk football. It's nostalgic stuff,
but it is a very real and very powerful emotion as well.

Not surprisingly, you can see the mythology of old Pittsburgh
most clearly in the local beer commercials. Rolling Rock and Iron
City beers run ads that tap into the Pittsburgh of the golden age.
Prominently featured in sepia or hazy focus are the old ethnic neighborhoods, the taverns, throngs of hard-hatted workers carrying lunch
pails coming from the mill—their bonding and camaraderie almost
palpable—shots of football games, a gritty running play by a team
that can only be the old Stillers.

Yes, it's cynical—tapping a myth to peddle the beer—and, yes,
it trivializes the real lives behind the images, but once again, you
can't miss the power and intensity of what those days were to those

men. The Rolling Rock spot ends with the poignant, untrue refrain "Same as it ever was . . ."

Arthur McEnery has always believed football was the important basis for Pittsburgh's mythology. "Years ago, back when the Stillers were a municipal embarrassment, the Pirates were a darned respectable major league baseball team. Many a Saturday and Sunday afternoon I'd pay my quarter, take the sun out in the bleachers, and watch the old Dutchman, Honus Wagner, and Pie Traynor and the Waner brothers and Arky Vaughan. But in its basic temperament, in its soul of souls, Pittsburgh is a football town, always was.

"I can't prove it, but football speaks more to the fiber of the people in this city than anything else. Even if the Stillers revert to the old days and become the league's doormat, this will stay a football town. Baseball, fine. But football *means* something here. Why? Darned if I know. Sometimes I swear I think it just comes right up out of the soil here."

In 1988, the baseball Pirates had their finest season in a decade. They finished second to the Mets in the National League East, with a young and improving team. They sold more tickets than ever before in their history, over two million. The 1988 Steelers, as noted, were abysmal. Yet every game at Three Rivers Stadium was sold out. They had, in fact, sold out for 119 consecutive games until the 1987 strike games broke the string. The Steelers have a request list for season tickets that will ensure sellouts for at least six more seasons.

The Pirates have proved that winning draws fans; the Steelers draw through winning and losing seasons. Of course, winning matters, but basically, it is the game itself that draws people in this place. If you doubt it, when Aliquippa plays archrival Ambridge, ten thousand spectators overflow a high school stadium with a capacity of eight thousand.

I've come to the same mysterious conclusion as Arthur McEnery: I honestly believe the football madness in western Pennsylvania really does "come right up out of the soil." Perhaps that's because I believe in the "Spirit of Place." The phrase belongs to the British novelist D. H. Lawrence, who came to America to search for the source of the power he admired in our literature. He wrote: ". . . different places on the face of the earth have different vital effluence, different vibrations . . . different polarity, call it what you like. But Spirit of Place is a great reality." There is something strangely physical and compelling in this western Pennsylvania landscape. Football does indeed come right up out of this ground.

My God, do they play football here. They have always played football here, or at least ever since there was football. The spirits of this place insist on it.

When America threw her gates wide open to immigrants at the end of the last century, it was because she needed strong shoulders to carry her to industrial prominence. The central furnace of her industrial greatness was hotly forged here of coal and iron and steel, in a blessed conjunction of people and geography. The people came from the mining regions in Poland, Germany, France, and all the Balkan countries. Irish, Italians, and Ukrainians came. There was hard work to be done here and payment for that work.

Two insights captured the essence of the place and the people. British writer James Parton described the place as "Hell with the lid off." Teddy Roosevelt said, "Pittsburgh has not been built up by talking about it. . . . There is not a Pittsburgh man who did not earn his success through his deeds."

When the damnable work was over, the sport those men played was soccer. They played it under the stacks, they played it under the coal tipples, they played it in fields behind their churches, they played it on cobblestone streets. But their kids played football. It was new and daring, like America. The kids wanted to be American kids.

They were big, heavy-thighed kids who were better at blocking and tackling than at the nimble-footed moves of European soccer. Football, as they first played it, was a bruising running game of courage and will, the style that was the hallmark of football in this region until the great quarterbacks began to develop in the towns along the rivers.

Kids shoot hoops from long range on playgrounds all over Indiana, and they bang the boards viciously in ghetto schoolyards of all the East Coast cities. Up in Minnesota, important high school hockey games draw more than eighteen thousand. Baseball, well, they play that everywhere, but more of it where the weather's better. They play all those sports in western Pennsylvania, but not the way they play football.

Last season in the NFL there were sixty players who hailed from an area within one hundred miles of Pittsburgh. No other region produces so much football talent in so concentrated a space. College scouts call it the "fertile crescent."

Football is not a sport here. It is a human ritual with a variety of crucial functions. Drive through a town like Jeannette, twenty miles east of Pittsburgh, and you see high school booster signs in every store on the main street, which becomes a lonely place on Friday night as soon as the lights flash on up at the field. The town is overwhelmingly Italian, and the men coming off the 5 P.M. shift at the glass factories will have a few drinks at the bar and talk about the great Italian players who have done Jeannette proud, foremost among whom is Dick Hoak, a Steelers running back for ten years and Noll's backfield coach for almost twenty.

They'll eventually walk up to the stadium, where about seven thousand parents and children and friends have already gathered. People other people have known all their lives are here. For those unfortunates working the night shift in the glass factories, the game is piped in over the loudspeaker system.

Football is a rite of passage, a trial by ordeal that comes at a time when boys are required to put aside the silliness of childish things and begin to act out the warrior ways of the men. Sacrifice and pain and courage, it is thought, will teach them to live better in their new, manly bodies. Football requires all those things.

It is a bonding rite, in the sense that every man-child on a high school team is not only joined to his teammates by valiant deed, but bound forever to all the boys who ever played on high school fields in western Pennsylvania on Friday night. More important, football links generations of men. A boy with a strong body doesn't have the choice of not playing football. A Pittsburgh man I know, reluctant to go out for the team when he was a boy, remembers telling his father, "If I was from some other place, I wouldn't have to play football." He still recalls his father's exact response: "You are not *from* some other place. You are from *this* place. My father played football. I played football. You will play football. And your sons will play football." He did indeed play. And so will his sons.

Football is also a rite of worship. The exceptional ones live in memory precisely as Alexander was remembered by the Macedonians; a blending of history and fable is absorbed into the haze of legend in the steel-mill towns along the rivers. The great ones are still immortal, their football deeds passed along by generations of fathers and sons. Not an accident, then, that Frank "Tiger" Walton and his boy, Joe, from up in Beaver Falls, became the first father and son to play in the National Football League. Joe coaches the New York Jets these days. And yes, that's the same town where Joe Willie Namath was the high school centerpiece on Friday nights, a place where no other quarterback seemed to exist.

In the cafés and saloons of the river towns, the feats of Johnny Lujack, from Connellsville, and Leon Hart, from Turtle Creek, have been reshaped and embellished since the late forties. Mike Ditka remains for the Slavic population in Aliquippa the closest thing to

Hercules on the face of the earth. John Unitas played quarterback at St. Justin's High in Mount Washington, a huge bluff that overlooks downtown Pittsburgh.

Har-Brack High School had a man-child running back in the early fifties who didn't even bother playing college ball: Cookie Gilchrist went right to the Cleveland Browns. His legend didn't blossom in Cleveland, but with the Buffalo Bills in the AFL. Cookie Gilchrist is the John Henry of western Pennsylvania.

Har-Brack was the same school that offered the NFL the Modzelewski brothers—Big Mo and Little Mo. Tony Dorsett may be at the end of a great NFL career, but don't dare say that in any bar in Hopewell. Not unless you want to get levitated right out the door by the glares of large men.

The legends live. Kids are weaned on them. Through oral history, the torch is passed. We play football here; we play great football here. And the process continues. Dan Marino, from Pittsburgh Central Catholic, Jim Kelly, from East Brady High, Joe Montana, from Monongahela, and Bernie Kosar, from just over the Ohio border in Youngstown, have inherited and enhanced the Lujack and Unitas and Namath quarterback legacies. They are already the models for ten-year-olds, whose fathers teach them to finger the laces of the ball with their eyes closed. Great football re-creates itself continually here, as ritual is layered upon myth.

Football is the rite of autumn that begins when the air turns chill in mid-September and intensifies when it is frigid in November. The greens turn to yellow and then to rust and wine, the dark earth blackens. The smell of decaying leaves hangs in the thin air, its odor so close to burning you look around for the smoke. The big boys come home from school, do their chores, and get ready to face their futures—and their pasts—on football fields, doing what boys have done here since the turn of the century. All the rituals come together on Friday nights in all the old mill towns along the Allegheny and

Monongahela rivers, along the Ohio even after it crosses out of Pennsylvania and into the foothills of Ohio and West Virginia.

Usually the Steelers have a number of players from the region, but in '88 there was only one, and he wasn't really a local boy. Chuck Lanza, a rookie third-round draft choice from Notre Dame, didn't get to play very much because he was Mike Webster's backup at center. Although Lanza played junior-high football in Coraopolis and would certainly have played in high school, where his father had played before him, his family moved to Tennessee in 1977 when he was thirteen. "My dad's business went bankrupt because the economy here was so bad back then," Chuck says, "and we had to move away. I'd have loved to have played around Pittsburgh." Chuck Lanza never got to live the rituals he'd heard so much about.

There is a new mythology being manufactured in Pittsburgh these days, one that is trying to exorcise the ghosts of the gritty past. Its refrain might be: "Forget what it ever was," and it is sung persistently by the Pittsburgh Chamber of Commerce, which proclaims the city completely transformed, a model for the nation on how to handle the wrenching economic changeover from ugly mill town to service-industry metropolis. From unpleasant to lovely. From dirty to clean. From granite to glass. From union to nonunion. From male to female. And, in a very elemental way, from the power of myth to the effectiveness of images.

The economic miracle, proudly called the "Pittsburgh Renaissance" in municipal literature, is projected most dramatically in the futuristic architecture of the downtown commercial towers that are clustered at the confluence of the Allegheny and Monongahela rivers and are known as the golden triangle. Yet another startling change—from rust to gold.

The brave new Pittsburgh proclaims itself in lots of other unmistakable ways as well. Arrive at Greater Pittsburgh International

Airport and you're hit by a large sign boasting, THE MOST LIVABLE
CITY IN AMERICA. Pick up your bags and there's another. And another at the taxi stand, and on and on.

Yes, Rand McNally has voted Pittsburgh "most livable," but why
the never-ending self-aggrandizement? Sure she's proud, but doesn't
she proclaim too much?

Nevertheless, it is a pleasure to see that the sky above western
Pennsylvania really is azure and to know you can breathe the air
without developing a regional wheeze. The rivers are cleaner—not
clean, clean*er*—and the line of ugly ore and coal barges has stopped.
Probably forever.

It is fair to say that no industrial city in America reflects the Old
Gipper's Reaganomics as directly as Pittsburgh does. The loss of
industrial lifeblood, in the form of jobs going to places in the world
where labor costs are significantly lower (and profits that much
higher), has not been stanched in the eighties; quite to the contrary,
the bleeding has been encouraged. Pittsburgh was given no choice;
it had to make a change or die. It is branded a "renaissance," an
"economic miracle," and its result is clean, modern, "livable" Pittsburgh. Look at the "miracle" closely, however, and you'll see it is
really sleight of hand, more illusion than substance, far more illusion.

The unemployment rate topped out at 16 percent in 1982 and
began to fall to what passes for acceptable these days, but the figures
deceive, as service-industry figures usually do. The new clerical jobs
at banks, investment firms, and insurance companies were filled
mostly by women at salaries only slightly above the minimum wage.

The younger laid-off mill hands tried to retrain themselves; those
who found jobs felt fortunate, even though they were poorly paid.
The older men collected unemployment for a while and eventually
went to the reduced pension benefits of early retirement. Both
groups remain bitter. The fast-food industry—among the top ten
employers in Pittsburgh now—pays teenagers and some older

women the minimum wage, and these jobs, too, are considered "employment," and they bear the same statistical weight as that of coal miner or open-hearth worker.

The employment figures for the city look respectable because one-job families became two- and three-job families, although together husband, wife, and kid rarely make as much as a single steelworker used to. The figures do not measure the pride and sense of dignity that go with actually bringing something tangible and useful into being, as opposed to moving paper around, tapping on a computer keyboard, sending smooth sounds over a telephone line, or flipping a quarter-pounder. "Most livable" came at an invisible cost that hasn't been totaled yet.

But the greatest deception has been the redefinition of what constitutes Pittsburgh itself. Pittsburgh of the steelmaking days was a region. Wherever the steel was made, that was Pittsburgh. The central city of the neighborhoods was supplemented by steel towns up and down the Allegheny, the Monongahela, the Ohio, and all the smaller tributaries, the ethnic towns that climbed sharply up the hills from the river mills—towns like Homestead, McKeesport, Duquesne, Braddock, Clairton, McKees Rocks, Frank Krupka's Aliquippa, Ambridge, and Beaver Falls, among dozens of others.

Conditions in these towns are every bit as bad as they were in the Great Depression, maybe worse. On the streets at midday, you see forlorn men—black or white, depending on which town or section of town—leaning against boarded-up storefronts. They have become invisible, no longer even unemployment statistics because their benefits have run out. Since they won't just go away, they are overlooked in the upbeat focus on "renaissance" and "most livable."

Aliquippa, Frank Krupka, Jr's original home, is one of the most devastated towns, and it has one of the most devastating high school teams. There is a connection: Football excellence and aggressiveness constitute a ticket out of the dead-end despair that stalks these desolate streets, and the boys who play football here grab at that ticket.

I drove through town early one Sunday morning before a Steelers game. The high school stadium and the houses on the hill nearby displayed red-and-black placards and large Quips schedules showing that the team was undefeated and was ranked number one in its class statewide. At the other end of town, just before the underpass that led to the all but abandoned steel mill, dozens of picket signs stood against the wall. A particularly large one, also in red and black, carried the Polish word for "Solidarity." The next sign said, WE ARE SOLIDARITY!

An intense and precise young man who reveres traditional Pittsburgh, Vic Ketchman, a local football writer, was my chief guide through the city and the Steelers' 1988 season, and I could not have been more fortunate. Born in the city thirty-seven years before, Ketchman has covered the Steelers since 1972, when the team became one of the league's elite squads.

Ketchman is very aware of the invisible forces that shaped this region and this football franchise. For him, the real Pittsburgh remains a ghostly spirit, not the golden triangle or gentrified neighborhoods with lovely boutiques.

"This is not basically a friendly town," he insists. "It's a good town with good people, but for the old-timers friendship was a slow thing. Distrust had to be overcome. They're trying to sell the easy smile and 'Have a Nice Day' around here now, but it comes from elsewhere, not from this place."

Once I asked him to reduce Pittsburgh to its absolute essence. We were in the Steelers' press box. Ketchman considered for a long time and said, "I'll bet you own the land your house sits on, but that's not the way it is in Pittsburgh. This town is different. You own the square footage but you only own the ground six feet down. The state retains the mineral rights to everything below that. Lots of these houses are built right over mine shafts. Hell, everyone knows his house could begin to disappear tomorrow night. We even have a name for a house sinking—we call it 'subsidence.' Think of living in a place like that!"

D. H. Lawrence and Arthur McEnery would have understood perfectly. Dynasties rise and dynasties fall. Egypt, Persia, Greece, Rome, the Pittsburgh "Stillers." Why not the homes of the people who once made this city, this region, so remarkably productive? They sink back into the spirit world below the earth, the very earth from which all power here had once emanated.

HELL RIGHT UP
OUT OF THE GROUND

Soon after he retired in 1983, Terry Bradshaw began to criticize Chuck Noll's coaching publicly, and he still hasn't stopped. In essence, Bradshaw said that Noll had become a football dinosaur, that the modern game had passed him by. But no coach had been to the mountaintop and come back down with so many silver footballs; nor had a Noll-coached team ever gotten to the Super Bowl and lost. So Bradshaw's bitter seeds did not find fertile ground, at least not at first.

But Noll's teams had begun to lose as often as they won. In fact, midway through the '88 season, the Steelers' won-lost record since their last Super Bowl was exactly 65-65. And when Bradshaw's career as a CBS network analyst and a sportscaster on the affiliate in Pittsburgh gave him an electronic pulpit, folks in Pittsburgh couldn't help but pay some attention.

When they were both big winners, their shared goals were sufficient for Bradshaw and Noll to tolerate one another, but the relationship was often strained. "I was a country boy, and he didn't like it," says Brad now. "I didn't study like Johnny Unitas. I was silly and I was immature—I know that. He humiliated me in public. I hated everything about Chuck Noll in my early years."

At the end of Bradshaw's career, when an elbow injury suddenly sapped the major league strength from his arm, Noll said, "Maybe it's time Mr. Bradshaw got on with his life's work." Still bristling about it, Bradshaw says, "All I wanted at the end was a kind word. . . . Well, Mr. Noll, maybe now it's time *you* get on with yours."

The incompatibility ran deeper than differences of personality. Noll's philosophy of football—or of life, for that matter—did not place a flamboyant quarterback in a central role.

Chuck Noll grew up in East Cleveland in the rock-bottom poverty of the Depression and played the game as a lineman at Dayton University and then as a "shuffling" guard on Paul Brown's Cleveland championship teams of the mid-fifties. He was a twenty-first-round draft choice who made it.

Football is for Noll an elemental game of control, and you control it offensively by running the ball. In his mind it is a matter, first and foremost, of blocking, running, tackling—elemental stuff performed in so crisp and punishing a manner that an opponent begins to doubt himself. Yes, even at this level of play there is such a thing as fear.

Noll also believes that ultimate control begins with defense, when an opponent realizes he is unable to do what he would like to do. Make him start to consider the cost/benefit ratio of running or catching a ball and you begin to win the mental battle. It is a point of honor with Noll that it all be done within the rules, but there is a gray area between aggressiveness and foul play that can't be controlled. Noll prefers to turn his players loose and leave that area to the officials.

There have been many excellent teams in football history but very few dynasties. The main difference between the two is not really how often they win games—it is *how* they win those games. Dynasty teams beat you and they beat you up; they do both with elemental execution.

It was never any secret to their opponents, for example, when

Lombardi's Packers would run their sweep or when Noll's traps
would set up Franco Harris into the middle. *Here it comes—try to
stop it!* Against dynasties, opponents know what is coming and still
can't do anything about it—that's the dynasty signature. The old
Yankees beat you with the long ball, the Celtics with superb passing
and defense; the Steelers simply controlled you.

Lynn Swann, an artiste among churls on the great Steelers teams
and one of Bradshaw's favorite passing targets, took his place among
the greatest receivers in football history when he retired in '82. Now
an ABC sportscaster, he remains an avid Noll watcher. "To understand Chuck's approach to offense, all you have to do is look at one
position: tight end. Back in 1975, we drafted a terrific tight end,
Walter White, from Maryland. Outstanding pass catcher. Chuck
cut the guy in training camp. Kansas City picked him up, he caught
a ton of passes, and he played in the Pro Bowl. In Chuck's system,
the tight end blocks. Period. And that tells you his priorities."

Once Noll has established his running game, he'll pass. And he'll
pass deep. Precisely because he has the bread and butter, he'll
surprise everybody by serving up a rich chocolate torte. That's when
Bradshaw's arm would fire the coup de grâce.

Even though he had the arm—and the receivers—to make the big
play at any time, Bradshaw also had an ego to fill Three Rivers, so
it always galled him that Noll saw what he did as finishing work. No
matter how glamorous the big throw looked to the fans, Noll seemed
to treat Bradshaw as though he were merely polishing off a product
other men had constructed.

Fun-loving, immature Terry Bradshaw was a talented, intuitive,
larger-than-life free spirit at quarterback—Babe Ruth playing football for Ebenezer Scrooge. His talent was so boundless that when the
team was going bad, when key players were hurt or the running game
was stymied, the Steelers could ride Bradshaw's arm (and Swann's
and Stallworth's remarkable hands) to win games in which they'd

been outplayed. And after Bradshaw did it, Noll was anything but effusive in his praise.

In the end, Brad felt that, successful as he had been, Noll's philosophy, and the man himself, had denied him the fullest measure of the appreciation he deserved. Hence the sniping when the dynasty collapsed. Whatever Bradshaw's motives, his criticism of Noll's coaching was valid, at least in the sense that he raised one irreducible question: Can Chuck Noll's basic philosophy still work in this day and age, when the NFL tries to impose parity by equalizing the talent?

Bradshaw has answered with an unequivocal no. "Let's face it," he says, "he won because he had superior players at almost every position. He can't do it without that edge." The Noll era, he contends, should have come to an end in 1986, after consecutive 7-9 and 6-10 seasons. The new, younger, more vital and imaginative regime would then have already had a rebuilding year under its belt and perhaps been a giant step closer to respectability when the 1988 training camp began.

Of course, there was absolutely no guarantee a new coach and philosophy would have been an improvement, but Bradshaw doesn't bother to address that.

The 1988 training camp began in a sizzling July, as usual. Hope sprang eternal, as usual. And, as usual, even a cautious man could find a basis for hope, but there were lots of contingencies attached. Optimism is such a natural, such a reasonable feeling in July. Of course, the skeptics were more certain than ever the downward spiral hadn't yet bottomed out.

Every team goes to camp with holes to be filled. Obviously, the fewer the holes, the better the chance of filling them. The Steelers had plenty of holes; it wasn't likely they'd be able to plug them all in camp. But teams had done it before when a large number of first- and second-year players made quantum leaps in technique and confidence at the same time and managed to stay relatively healthy. It was also possible for the coaches to make some adjustments in tactics in order to minimize or "hide" a few of the holes.

Realists know, however, that a football team suffers an enormous amount of wear and tear over the course of an average season. In the NFL, durability, or "depth," is a most vital element. Having enough quality backups and good players who can double at other positions is a common denominator of all top-echelon teams.

Not only did they have significant holes to fill, but the Steelers were thin even where the fabric was not actually torn. In most of the positions where the Steelers had good players they didn't have proven second-line players, and while a durable team has the chance of overcoming injuries, a thin team can be torn to shreds by midseason. Therefore a thin team must stay healthy, but no team can count on that; in fact, most of the time you can count on just the opposite.

Noll's problems, then, were three: Fill the holes; get more production out of the proven players; and improve the quality of the reserves. As it had been each July for twenty years, St. Vincent College was where Chuck Noll would start to solve his problems.

Noll's camps are generally understood to be demanding but fair. Not the all-out war of attrition of a martinet like Frank Gansz at Kansas City, for example, where the ones left standing at the end make the team. They're more like Vince Lombardi's camps, where the annual reintroduction to pain was tempered by a respect for the individuals enduring that pain. Says Noll, "The object of football is not to break men's bodies and spirits; it's to win football games."

In 1988, for the first weeks until the preseason games began, there were hard two-a-day practices, an early-morning session, when the heat was bearable, and a 3 P.M. practice, when it wasn't. Between the two there was time for lifting weights, eating, napping, and a bit of study with the playbook. There was almost always a team meeting after dinner until around 9 P.M.

A lights-out curfew was at eleven, and the rooms were checked by an assistant coach. Most of the time it was Joe Greene. There weren't any great curfew stories like the time they managed to get Bradshaw to miss it against his will, and he got caught and fined. "This group of young lions," Greene said, "is sure a lot tamer than in the old days."

Some concessions were made to veterans. Their rooms were in the rear of the dormitory, the side that got less oppressive early sun and was shaded by trees. Although the rooms were a bit cooler, they also overlooked an old graveyard, which could have had symbolic significance to players fighting for their jobs. All rooms were Spartan and exactly the same: two cots, two desks, two small chests, two closets, one ceiling light. A border of bricks ran across the ceiling of every room; like prisoners, the players memorized the exact number—seventeen.

Most of the players doubled up; an occasional veteran who wanted some privacy, like Mike Webster, had the option of being alone. As the camp wore on, more and more double rooms became singles. The ball boy who acted as the training camp's Turk would rap on a door, call a player's name, and say, "Modrak wants to see you. Bring your playbook." It was the end.

Tom Modrak, the Steelers' director of pro scouting, was also in charge of training-camp operations. When the staff agreed to cut a player, Modrak was the man who bore the news. He took the playbook and gave him his final check. Veterans got better treatment. Generally they didn't get cut till later in camp, and when they did, Noll sat them down for a fuller explanation. The result was the same, though; they'd been Turked.

During their rare free nights, and especially on Saturday, almost everyone flew out of the dorm, the players to Bobby Dale's, a bar on Route 30 near Latrobe, the coaches and writers heading in the opposite direction, to Pete's near Greensburg. Bobby Dale's is flashier and draws a younger, dancing, action-oriented crowd. Pete's is a threadbare tavern, perfect for reflective imbibing.

The curfew did not apply to coaches. And it most assuredly did not apply to the writers. The best story to come out of the 1988 camp featured Myron Cope, who is unequivocally the most popular sportscaster in Pittsburgh, an institution, in fact, and his pal Norm Vargo, a writer for the *McKeesport Daily News.*

Cope was driving; rather, he was behind the wheel. One of the problems with their finding their way back to St. Vincent on a straight line was that Cope is diminutive and had trouble seeing out over the hood; the other was that he'd been at Pete's until 2 A.M. Vargo talked him back to the general vicinity and finally brought them up the long entranceway to the school. Cope drove straight for the security guard's booth, only at the last minute avoiding it. Then he stopped, rolled down his window, looked for some coins in his pocket, and tried to pay the toll.

Vargo told the story the next morning and it quickly swept the camp. Noll, who seemed to like Myron, or was at least amused by him, particularly enjoyed the story and told it to everyone who hadn't heard it, which was quickly no one whatsoever at St. Vincent.

July and August 1988 were the hottest in Latrobe in living memory. It was so hot on average nationally, in fact, that the Senate held emergency hearings in Washington to determine the relationship between the thinning ozone layer and the heating up of the planet. In Latrobe it felt like the sun was falling right through the ozone.

It was John Jackson's first camp. Jackson, an offensive lineman, who, like Aaron Jones, was out of Eastern Kentucky, but, unlike Jones, a lowly tenth-round draft choice, was fighting for his football life. "Morning workouts were tough, yeah, but the afternoons were the killers. The damn grass got hot. It was like hell was coming right up out of the ground." In those terms, Chuck Noll must have seemed like the Devil himself.

For Frank Pollard, the fullback, it was the tenth camp. Because he had been hard used in his career and required two knee operations in '86, Pollard was battling to make the team. A friendly, agreeable man, he always minimized the pressures and discomforts of the camp. "Man's got to do what he's got to do" was a standard, smiling retort to most questions about how tough the practices were. "Personally, I kind of like it hot. Sweats the evil fluids out of your system. This heat's not too bad. I'm a Texas boy."

Texas boy he may have been, but no one associated with the Steelers could remember a camp so infernally and consistently parched. This heat burned the backs of the players' legs; it scorched their nostrils; it dehydrated a few and broke more than a few spirits.

"One of the reasons some guys have such a tough time with camp," said Joe Greene, who had been through sixteen of them as player and coach, "is they think of it as a physical ordeal, and it is. But it's not only that; it's a mental thing as well. It's a time for thinking, a time to put your mind in control."

A man who did that successfully was Tunch (pronounced "Toonch") Ilkin, one of the team's co-captains. He found the camp "real hot, sure. And sure, Chuck pushed us but, hell, that's a Chuck Noll training camp."

Tunch is a living testament to the triumph of positive thinking. He came to the Steelers from Indiana State in the sixth round, an undersized lineman with the slimmest of chances to make the team, but he fit Noll's standards for a trapping lineman—quick, intelligent, gutsy (probably very like Noll himself as a player)—and he stuck, but very marginally at first. Ilkin had willed and worked himself hard enough to become one of the league's best offensive tackles. The 1988 training camp was his ninth as a Steeler.

It should have been Mike Merriweather's seventh camp. A three-time Pro Bowl selection, he was at the peak of his career and one of the only bona fide stars on the team. At the end of the '87 season, after being selected the team's Most Valuable Player, Merriweather insisted on renegotiating his contract. The '88 season was to be the next-to-last year of a five-year agreement.

Football, more than any other professional sport, is a buyer's market. Team owners, through a variety of means whose legitimacy is still to be determined by the courts, have managed to maintain control of how and where most players can sell their services. The Steelers, with the lowest payroll in the twenty-eight-team league last season, have often stated their policy on contract renegotiation. As clarified by Joe Gordon, the team's business manager, it is: "We do not renegotiate." Legally, their position was impeccable—*Man signs three-year contract; man is bound by three-year contract.*

But emotion and common sense should come into play in such matters as well. Mike Merriweather had been a model employee and one hell of a linebacker for six years. Around the league, star line-backers like Lawrence Taylor, Andre Tippett, and Wilber Marshall were making more than $1 million a year. Merriweather had con-tracted for $300,000 per annum with $50,000 in performance bonuses.

The Steelers' brass understood Merriweather's frustration. "When those other guys made their contracts public," said Gordon, "it became for Mike a matter of pride and ego as much as anything else." The Steelers did not want to hard-line him; on the other hand, they would not alter their no-renegotiation policy and open the contractual floodgates. Dan Rooney was not completely unreason-able; he offered a two-year contract extension at $1.2 million. Mer-riweather's agent demanded $1 million a year.

Since the Steelers were making the right gestures, even if not offering the right numbers, everyone assumed the linebacker would sign before too long. What choice did he have, really? If he didn't accept the Steelers' extension offer, there was nowhere else he could sell his services, unless the Steelers decided to trade him. Some shrewdly cynical writers believed that was his agent's strategy from the outset. Merriweather's alternative was to sit out the season and lose both the whole year's income and a prime season of his athletic life.

A trade was unlikely on three counts. First, it was doubtful the Steelers would receive true value since they would be dealing under duress. Second, a dangerous precedent might be set, encouraging other unhappy players to force management's hand in the same manner. Third, most owners and general managers around the league just didn't feel comfortable making trades. Trades are a staple of professional baseball; no-trades are a staple of professional football. Some call it collusion.

When Merriweather did not attend training camp, fans and reporters alike assumed the impasse would break in a week or two. Merriweather was always in excellent shape; it wouldn't take long for him to get used to contact again. By the second or third preseason game, he'd be the Mike Merriweather the Steelers defense was counting on.

Merriweather never played a down for the Steelers in 1988. He opted for the unthinkable, and depending on your point of view, he was either a proud and highly principled young man or a damn fool who gambled on the advice of a bad agent and lost.

Although injury did not strike down unusually large numbers of players in the Steelers' 1988 camp, it did pick out the worst possible victims. In a scrimmage on the third day of practice, Keith Willis, the team's best defensive lineman, got hurt in a simple head-butting drill linemen use to accustom their heads, necks, and shoulders to full contact. It was a familiar pain, a shock to a nerve players call a "burner." Usually it stings like hell for a while before it gradually passes. Not in Willis's case. It was diagnosed a herniated disc. The microsurgery that ensued finished the lineman's season.

Coupled with Merriweather's holdout, almost nothing could have been worse for the defense. Willis and Merriweather were the pressure men, each having led the team in quarterback sacks in two of the previous four seasons. Their effectiveness rippled out to other players; if offenses keyed on those two, other Steelers were able to make big plays.

With Willis pressuring from the left side and Merriweather blitzing from his linebacker position, Aaron Jones would have a better chance to develop into the rusher the scouts and coaches had anticipated. Without them, Jones would be on his own, in essence thrown to the wolves.

The injury count didn't end with Willis. Delton Hall fractured his wrist in a scrimmage the second week of camp. But because there were so many injuries in the defensive backfield, Noll didn't have the luxury of sitting him down. So he appeared briefly, at least, in most of the games, though he and the team might have been better off had he been kept out; he was barely a shadow of his former self.

Normally the key to Hall's effectiveness was the blow he delivered with his hands to a wide receiver at the line of scrimmage. Playing now in great pain, with a soft cast on his wrist, took away his ability to control an opponent with his initial bump.

At his best Hall wasn't so much a cornerback as a throwback—to Mel Blount and Donnie Shell, incredible hitters in the open field. If a receiver chose to go over the middle to make a catch, he knew he would be made to pay for it. A Delton Hall smack in 1987 made eyebrows go up along the sidelines, a gasp roll down from the stands, and brought a thin smile to Chuck Noll's lips. Because he was forced to play hurt and reinjured the wrist continually in 1988, Delton Hall didn't have a classic pop all year. And as the season wore on, he wore down psychologically; he was a shaken, sullen athlete most of the time. By season's end, his confidence was as shattered as his wrist.

If someone had planned to cripple the Steelers' defense by throwing darts at the key names on their depth chart, it would have been impossible to do more damage than what happened by chance.

Willis, Merriweather, and Hall were the three most indispensable parts of a good NFL defense on the verge of becoming very good. Instead, that defense would disintegrate.

There were the usual number of injuries on offense also, but none so serious it forced major alterations. Then there were the truly odd occurrences. For example, quite unannounced one day, starting guard John Rienstra packed and left camp. "Rhino," as his teammates called him, had been selected in the first round in 1986, the ninth player chosen overall. His size, strength, work ethic, and potential made him a blue-chip prospect. What could not have been anticipated was his tendency toward extreme introspection. Rhino tried to be too perfect, and while that drove him to excel, it also caused him to dwell morbidly on every mistake until he lost perspective, which in turn caused him to lose a good football player's main virtue—instinctive response.

Rhino had bleeding stomach ulcers for years, but they worsened right before camp. Everyone believed that he had been dealing pretty well with the problem, but then suddenly he disappeared.

Apparently the ulcers had been acting up again. Although his teammates saw little of him over the next two weeks, he did contact the front office. He was put in touch with a therapist, who helped Rhino realize his chief problem wasn't football, but the pressures he put on himself.

When he returned to camp, many of his teammates were sympathetic and encouraging. But grizzled old-timers shook their heads in disbelief. One said, "If Rhino couldn't block a bulldozer, you think they'd have babied him the way they have? Hell, in the old league, they'd have whipped his ass right into shape—or shipped him out."

As the heat of July simmered, Noll knew his need to fill the holes and develop better backup players really meant getting rid of veterans. Every time he was queried about cuts, he said they'd be made on a case-by-case basis, but there seemed to be an underlying selection principle: Players with potential were selected over those with accomplishments past and present. Among the more prominent veterans, running back Walter Abercrombie, nose tackle Gary Dunn, and linebacker Robin Cole got Turked. Collectively, they'd given the Steelers twenty-three good seasons, some downright excellent ones in Cole's case.

This made sense in purely financial terms since the savings to the Steelers was enormous: Those three players made around $1 million collectively, their replacements about a third that much. But while money was, as usual, a consideration, it was not the motivation. The veterans, their best years behind them, could only supply adequacy, not excellence. The Steelers opted to go with younger, untried players in hopes of finding some future stars.

Abercrombie caught on with the Philadelphia Eagles and Cole with the New York Jets; Dunn retired from football. The survivors breathed a collective sigh of relief. Pollard, who had been right on the margin, said, "When you see guys you've known all these years go, you get a double sort of feeling. You hurt like heck for them. And you're secretly glad for yourself but you try not to show it, 'cause you know it could be you, *will* be you someday. In a way, it is you, too, if you know what I mean. For a few days afterward, you got to remind yourself it's not."

Ilkin, whose job was never really in jeopardy but who knew all the insecurities fostered by the business of professional football, looked back at what he had once again survived and sighed. "There are so many pitfalls just to get a chance to play in this league, you can't believe them. Every season new, young, big kids come along and try to take your job away. And if you survive that, one wrong hit can finish your season. Just look at Keith [Willis]. And on top of all that there's heat that fries guys' brains. I'm sure glad it's over."

In the preseason games, youth and enthusiasm compensated for the team's shortcomings. In their first exhibition against the defending Super Bowl champion Washington Redskins on a Monday night in

August, the Steelers gave their wishful thinkers something tangible—a 44–31 victory. Bubby Brister, who had won the starting job early in camp from an inconsistent Todd Blackledge, threw long very well. Warren Williams, a rookie from Miami University, flashed breakaway running speed some Pittsburgh fans couldn't remember seeing before. A preseason win in August is a long way from the playoffs, but there were so many first- and second-year players doing well, only a spoilsport would be critical.

The following week they did it again, surprising the Eagles 21–16. It was accomplished on a nice second-half comeback by young players fighting like hell for jobs. Again, the win didn't count, but Noll was trying to make believers out of players who weren't sure they could cut it, and winning any time, in any way, can establish a foundation of belief.

The bubble burst the following week, when the New York Giants beat the Steelers 28–17. In the parlance of the game, the Giants just "kicked ass." Welcome to the NFL, boys.

Just before the Giants game, Art J. Rooney, Sr.—the beloved "Chief"—suffered a stroke in his Three Rivers office, the one with the steel-gray carpeting and dozens of photos of his favorite players. He had long ago passed most of the organizational responsibilities to his eldest son, Dan, the team president.

Art Rooney died in his sleep in Mercy Hospital a few days before his Steelers were to play their last preseason game. He was eighty-seven. Most of those years were lived generously, thoughtfully, and with great style. It is doubtful if even Fred Rogers ("Mr. Rogers"), whose program emanated from WQED, Pittsburgh's educational station, was more appreciated as a caring human being in Pittsburgh.

The Chief's greatest quality was authenticity. He never was other than a North Side neighborhood guy. Until it became too much for him a few years ago, he would walk the half-mile from his many-gabled Victorian house on North Lincoln Street to Three Rivers.

Much of the North Side has gone to seed by now; with the exception of North Lincoln and a few other well-tended streets, it has the general look of Rust Belt neglect. A great many unemployed men, most of them black, cluster on street corners. The houses lean over in disrepair. Trash fills the empty lots and spills out to the curbs. Art Rooney was always seen by the people who live here as a neighborhood treasure, a vestige of the best qualities of an earlier time.

Everyone in Pittsburgh knew Art Rooney stories, or at least versions of them: the youthful boxer and football player; the middle-aged dandy and gambler who parlayed a hot day at the track into an NFL franchise; the mature promoter who kept one of the worst football teams in history in the town he loved until his luck turned and his team became the best team ever.

Joe Greene recalled first meeting Mr. Rooney the year he was drafted by the Steelers. "I was the first player picked by the Steelers in the draft, and I didn't think they were making me a fair offer, so I came on up to negotiate. I was there a few days and Mr. Rooney came by and asked what I was doing in the office all the time. 'Trying to sign my contract,' I said. 'What's the problem?' he asked. 'We're ten thousand dollars apart.' Mr. Rooney's eyes twinkled in that way he had and he waved his big cigar. 'Give it to him,' he said to his son. 'He's worth it.' That easy gesture made me want to be worth it, whether I was or not."

Every chance he could, Mean Joe sat in the Chief's office and listened to stories about the old days. Racetrack stories about characters named Bet-a-Million Gates and Swifty Morgan, old fight yarns about matches he promoted in Forbes Field, memories of the diverse sporting events he got involved in over the years. "Whatever that man talked about," Joe said, "I took it as part of my education. I had me a wonderful teacher."

Funeral services were held at St. Peter's, Art Rooney's North Side church. A steady rain broke the summer heat. There was a clause in the Chief's will that stipulated his funeral could cost no more than $1,000. It was not observed.

The street in front of the church was thronged with more than a thousand mourners. Every former player in the area and many who chose to come to Pittsburgh paid their respects. Even though everyone knew an eighty-seven-year-old could not have been expected to endure many more years, no one wanted it to end this year. Or next year. Or the year after that. Among the people paying their respects was seventy-eight-year-old Arthur McEnery, who had taken the bus over from his apartment in Oakland.

Pittsburgh came to a standstill and grieved. All flags were dropped to half-staff. Newspapers ran anecdotes about the Chief. Every local TV and radio show recapitulated his remarkable life and paid homage to the good man, whose life reflected much of the history and carried the soul of this unique town he once described as "a middle place between here and there, but not akin to anywhere."

Steelers players, coaches, and members of the media boarded buses at Three Rivers Stadium and stopped at St. Peter's on the way to the airport, where their charter would take them directly to their game in New Orleans. Among the mass of mourners was an unexpected visitor waiting to pay his respects: Mike Merriweather. His presence gave rise to hopes that the contract stalemate would soon be broken.

On a small card passed out at the funeral was this simple poem, taken from an anonymous tombstone in Ireland:

> *Remember, man,*
> *As you pass by,*
> *That as you are*
> *So once was I,*
> *That as I am,*
> *So will you be,*

> *Remember, man,*
> *Eternity.*

These words were placed on the Chief's tombstone as well.

There was a fair amount of "Win one for the Chief" sentiment when the Steelers took the field at the Superdome. Even though very few of these young players could have known him very well, they knew of him, and that was enough to motivate them. Trailing 21–0 early, the Steelers closed to 28–14. The defense shut the Saints down in the fourth quarter, and Brister, playing professional football in his home state before friends who'd come down to the Big Easy from Monroe, helped the Steelers score two more touchdowns and moved them to field-goal position with less than two minutes left, winning it 31–28.

It was the game that made Bubby. He threw for 313 yards and three touchdown passes on national television.

Ed Bouchette, the beat writer for the *Pittsburgh Post-Gazette*, recalled Joe Greene saying afterward, "No doubt about it, the Chief was there, helping us out with this one."

FIREMAN 36 OR 37

GAME DAY 1: SUNDAY, SEPTEMBER 4

Dallas (0-0) at Pittsburgh (0-0)

Young black men are crowding the ramps that lead to the parking lots surrounding Three Rivers. They wave clusters of tickets at slowly rolling cars.

"How much?" I'm just curious.

"Thirty." The tickets are stamped $20. This Sunday is warm and sunny. The game is, as always in Pittsburgh, a sellout. The asking price is testament both to human optimism at the start of a new football season and to the law of supply and demand.

The parking lots are three quarters filled two hours before the game. It is, for the most part, a working-class (even though some are unable to find work), salt-of-the-earth, beer-drinking crowd. There aren't many credit cards in these nondesigner jeans. Charcoal smells waft on the warm air; burgers and franks sizzle on grills. Men and boys in Steelers jerseys toss footballs and run patterns between long rows of cars, vans, and pickup trucks. The baseball season still has more than a month to go.

I pull my car alongside a blue Chevy Blazer and lock it carefully. Behind me, a gruff voice says, "See a lot of them on the road these days. How's it drive?"

"I can't really say. Just rented it coming in from the airport."

Frank Krupka, Sr., is extending an aluminum lawn chair to its stress limit. He's wearing a Steelers jersey with Mean Joe Greene's number—75. He doesn't smile. He isn't exactly what you'd call friendly. He wants to talk, though. "Want a beer?"

It's a chilled Iron City, a bottle. I'm sweating. There are some Pittsburgh officials I want to talk to, my game credentials to pick up, a place in the press box to claim, and some newspaper friends to meet, but I'm here to write about a team, a town, and its people. "Sure."

Krupka does not introduce me to his wife, who is priming the grill behind the Blazer and peeking at me from time to time when she thinks I'm not looking. We talk football awhile and Krupka says, "If you're writing a book, you ought to talk to my Frankie. He knows all there is to know about the Stillers, lives and dies with them. Me, I like to see them win, but I really just want to see good football." And what constituted good football for Krupka? "Smart and brave." *Brave* is a surprising word to hear applied to professional football. I ask about it. "Short of war," he explains, "nothing is as threatening to the body and so testing to the nerves."

And what exactly does he expect from this year's team? "Well, we're just about starting from scratch again, so there's no telling. The marines say, 'We're looking for a few good men.' That's what I'm looking for too, and we'll build from there. I'm a Noll man, so I think it'll be all right. The thing that worries me, though, is why he waited so long to get rid of the dead weight. He should have done this years ago."

Frank Krupka's wife brings me an oversized hamburger smothered in onions. Krupka calls her "the missus."

"So when will this book of yours come out?" he asks.

"Next season."

He looks puzzled. "Why would anyone buy a book about a season after everyone knew how the Stillers did?"

"It won't be so much about *what* happened to the Steelers as it will about *how* and *why* it happened. And what it all means to the players and the people of Pittsburgh."

Krupka gets a strange look in his eye, as though he's talking to an idiot. "How you plan to begin this book?"

"I'm not sure—maybe with D. H. Lawrence."

"Who's he, a new linebacker?"

Before I leave, I ask Frank Krupka if he parks in this spot all season and if I could meet him here before the home games. He agrees. I say thank-you and good-bye to the missus, who looks at me narrowly.

Dallas vs. Pittsburgh. Landry vs. Noll. There was a time when such an opener would have highlighted an entire season. Not anymore. The Steelers haven't made the playoffs since 1984, the Cowboys since 1982, when sixteen teams were allowed into a postseason tournament. Both Noll and Landry know what sorts of teams they have, but they do not know how they will play. No one does. The Vegas bookies have made the Steelers a three-point favorite, primarily on the basis of home-field advantage.

All game long, the Cowboys move the football farther and more consistently than the Steelers. But professional football is big plays made at crucial moments, not yardage totals. This game can be distilled to three crucial plays.

The Steelers lead 10–7 with about a minute to go in the first half. The ball is a yard and a half away from the Cowboys' goal line and it is fourth down for the Steelers. Conventional wisdom, especially for a percentage coach like Noll, is to go for the automatic field goal and a 13–7 halftime lead. But hold everything. Brister calls time out, runs to the sideline, and initiates an animated conversation with Noll and offensive coordinator Tom Moore. What's happening here is incredible: The upstart quarterback is debating the curmudgeon coach.

Noll finally realizes this is not merely a situational decision, but one that will send a signal to a team that is still searching for its personality. (Later Noll admitted to the press, "Bubby influenced me. If you have a guy who thinks he can do it, you have to recognize that." Mouths fell open.)

Back on the field, Bubby calls Warren Williams's number into the middle on a trap. It isn't even close: Williams is piled up back on the 2.

The second-guessing throughout the stadium is loud and immediate, led by Myron Cope, the veteran color man on the Steelers' radio network. As soon as the Steelers had rejected the field-goal option and begun to line up for a running play, Cope made his disagreement perfectly clear all over western Pennsylvania and into West Virginia and Ohio. "That is not Chuck Noll. I can't believe that. That is a classic *dummkopf* call, Noll. They pick up only a yard and a half on three running plays, so what makes them think they'll get another yard and a half on fourth down? Of course the fans cheer when you go for it, but they forget those other guys out there trying to stop you. It's like they don't even exist. No, no, it's a *dummkopf*."

The second big play is an incredible Cowboys mistake that preserves the Steelers' lead. With about three minutes left in the game, and still trailing by just three points, the Cowboys drive to the Steelers' 4-yard line and appear to be going in for an easy touchdown. During his conference with quarterback Steve Pelluer, Coach Landry calls this play: *Fireman 37 fullback short rover curl*. Back in the huddle, Pelluer, who had been knocked slightly groggy on the previous carry, repeats: "Fireman thirty-six fullback short rover curl." The one-digit difference means that fullback Tim Newsome, the primary receiver, lines up in the wrong place and will run a different route. On the snap, Pelluer rolls to the right; the rest of the Cowboys flow to the left—a complete screwup. Pelluer, unprotected and under pressure, throws the ball right at David Little's numbers. Little plays for the Steelers. On such human miscommunication are NFL games lost—and won.

The Cowboys are not finished, however. They have a last-ditch drive, still three points behind, with the ball on the Pittsburgh 23 with fifty-three seconds left. A field goal will tie; a touchdown will almost certainly win. On a third-down pass play, Aaron Jones, who has been neutralized most of the game, takes a long, fast first step off the line of scrimmage; he gets his shoulder below the blocker's arm, explodes up and past him, and throws Pelluer to the artificial turf. Aaron has recorded his first NFL sack at the most opportune moment. A likely field goal has become a questionable 49-yarder. When it is finally attempted, it is short. Steelers win!

Drawls wide-eyed Aaron afterward about his rush: "I would not, I refused to be denied on that play. 'No matter what happens, Aaron,' I told myself, 'you're gonna get there this time.' Y'all saw what happened."

Buried in the game statistics—what Noll likes to call "the history of a football game"—there are some promising indicators, which, if maintained throughout the season, could result in a successful football team: *Pittsburgh, fumbles lost—0; Cowboys, interceptions by—0.* In other words, no Steelers turnovers.

Counting the preseason, the Steelers have won four out of five. The wins haven't been particularly handsome, but they are still wins. And they've done it all without Merriweather and Willis, with people playing hurt, with inexperienced players at key positions. Things are good and promise to get even better. But confidence is not yet there. Except for Brister and Jones, who are larger-than-life optimists, this team is mostly made up of quiet individuals. Maybe they are just being prudent, waiting to see if they are really as good as their record indicates.

About his game against the Cowboys, Aaron says, "Yeah, I got a whole lot of confidence out there today. I saw I could play in the National Football League." His eyes widen as he looks directly at my notebook. "Play," he repeats.

During the first half, after Ed "Too Tall" Jones deflected a pass, he ran into Bubby pretty hard, and the two exchanged some angry words. I ask Bubby what happened. Bubby says, "I can only tell you my part of the conversation. It was, 'Nice play, Mr. Too Tall . . . sir." Bubby is ecstatic about winning the opener: "I'll look in the paper tomorrow and read how lucky we were to win and about everything I did wrong. Then I'll turn to the league standings and see we're one-and-oh. I'll smile and smile."

If there had been any kindness in the computer that made up the NFL schedule, the Steelers would have played another team at about the same level as the Cowboys, or maybe a slight notch above. But the Steelers drew an away game against the defending Super Bowl champs, the Washington Redskins. How did Bubby feel about that? "So Washington's the champs. Hell, bring 'em on."

On a more timely note, Noll dismisses his team's preseason victory over the Skins as irrelevant: "When we played Washington then, they were still celebrating their Super Bowl. It won't be the same, I assure you."

In the darkening parking lot, six large men, each with Iron City bottles in their mitts, each wearing some Steelers garment, are pitching half-dollars. The closest to a crack in the asphalt ten yards away takes the pot. I watch awhile.

"Want to get in?" one of them asks.

I shake my head.

"Why not? You might get as lucky as the Stillers."

Lucky, perhaps, but as I go to my car, I smile at the fact that the

Steelers awarded the game ball to Dan Rooney in honor of the Chief.

For the true football fan, the impromptu discussion between Myron Cope and Noll at the latter's Monday press conference, is found gold. Cope asks Noll to compare the Cowboys' Herschel Walker to Jim Brown, the Cleveland Browns' immortal.

Noll used to block for Brown, or try to; Brown recalls having to yell for Noll to get out of the way. Noll begins conventionally: "You can't really compare them. Herschel has a unique ability—it's called four-point-two speed. You have to use a little bit of Pythagoras on him; that is, you have to get the 'right' angle. Herschel puts the shoulder into you. Jimmie Brown ran straight up and down and bowled you over with his thigh. You're not supposed to be able to do that. He was the strongest runner I ever saw."

THE FLIES

Legend has it that the great baseball umpire Bill Klem once was very late calling a pitch behind the plate.

"Foot outside," the hitter screamed.

"On the corner," the catcher opined.

"Gentlemen, a pitch doesn't even exist till I make the call," Klem explained.

Klem's is a significant statement when applied to modern life. It says that reality isn't important; what is important is the perception and interpretation of reality. In other words, power rests with those making the calls. For better or worse, in our world, the media makes the call.

The popularity of professional football, and accordingly, a great deal of its financial success, has been enhanced if not created by media attention. It has helped make the game a cultural ritual and put money in the pockets of just about everyone connected with the business. On balance that seems to be a pretty good thing, but in its power to make the call it can make or break careers. Consequently, most coaches and players are wary of journalists; they worry about that dangerous combination of power and the tendency to get the call dead wrong. In some classic cases, distrust has grown into paranoia.

Much of the time, the interests of the sports journalist and the professional athlete are different, and often downright incompatible. I've always been more sympathetic to the athlete's side of the contention, which, because the player isn't always articulate and hasn't direct access to the public, hardly ever gets told.

Tunch Ilkin—ironically, one of the players who knows his way around and through the media—depicts the player's lot as well as anyone. "The people who write about how we perform under tough game conditions," he says, "really have no idea what is actually going on out there, what we're trying to accomplish individually or as a team on a specific play or over the course of a game. Yet what those people write can affect a guy's career. I'm not saying they're all totally ignorant, but they just don't know what we know; still, they make judgments that shape fans' attitudes. And they are not completely objective—if they like a guy because he's good copy or feeds them inside stuff, they treat him well; if they don't, they'll dump on him."

Most players keep such sentiments to themselves. In their no-win situation, too much criticism of the media sounds like sour grapes. But basically it is the valid complaint the participant has about the nonparticipant. In this case, though, the nonparticipant holds all the power.

Players and writers are very different kinds of men. There's an old distrust between them that usually starts back in high school, where the athletes are the privileged ones, the golden boys who get the girls and the attention while the writers are grinding out English papers in dull obscurity and making fools of themselves in gym class. The gulf widens in college. Athletes become even more golden, with more and even flashier girls, acclaim, and few or no academic responsibilities. Journalism and communication majors look on the athletes' shimmering privileges from a gloomy and considerable distance.

I've noticed two basic types of jealous men in the media: the fellow who envies the athlete and wants to bask in his reflected aura—the vicarious type; and the resentful nerd, who is secretly glad to see the golden boy humbled, and, if need be, to do a little of the humbling himself.

Negativism or "getting the call wrong" in the media can be particularly disruptive to a football team because football is a team game unlike any of the others. There is a physical dependency of one man on another—not only for success but for survival—that cannot be fully understood by nonparticipants. Blending and maintaining team chemistry is very difficult because not every player benefits equally from success; players at glamour (the so-called skill) positions get most of the attention and the salary, but they rely for their accomplishment and well-being on anonymous bodies, men whose tempers and careers are usually nasty, brutish, and short.

Loose lips sink ships; they can disintegrate a football team. Players know that and are reluctant to give any ammunition to writers they do not trust. But there's a complication: Professional football depends on media attention to keep itself in the public's consciousness. Organizations want the ink, the words, the electronic pictures; they want their coaches and players seen and heard. So the athlete gets squeezed into another no-win situation.

Of all the teams in the league, none has more of an open-door—or open-locker-room—policy toward the press than the Steelers. It is Art Rooney's legacy and reflects the Chief's personality and his inclination from the old days to let his town know all about his team. Like Mr. Rooney himself, what you see is what you get.

Joe Gordon was for eighteen seasons the Steelers' publicity director, one of the most popular in the league, until he took over as business manager in 1987. He says, "I've always believed in Mr.

Rooney's approach to the press in this town, and I'm glad Dan has continued it. We've never tried to hide anything. We don't shield anyone from reporters. It's good for the players to face them. They have to learn to think on their feet, and that helps them get ready for life after football."

On most teams the quarterback gets the lion's share of attention, and his ability to handle it wisely and well is one of the skills teammates and management expect of him. It was particularly interesting to see Bubby Brister handle the press after the Dallas win. He was nonchalantly colorful, quotable, and informative. Brister has the chance of winning over the Pittsburgh media as convincingly as he has his teammates, many of whom believe he'll quarterback here for a decade.

A writer, scribbling in his book, said, "Bubby, let's say that call where you went for the TD on fourth down instead of taking the field goal had cost you guys the ball game. What would you be saying about it right now?" Nothing wrong with the question; all probes are valid.

Bubby drew himself up to full height and glared down at his questioner, establishing for a moment his physical dominance. Nothing wrong with that either. "You people amaze me. What the hell is it about you guys makes you so shit-negative all the time? We *won* a damn football game today and you ask a question about losing! You got some shit-negative head, you know that?"

No, "shit-negative" is not a Louisiana regionalism; it's a Bubbyism that came on the spur of the moment.

Naturally, Noll isn't as enthusiastic about the ever-increasing power of the media, in society in general as well as around the Steelers' Three Rivers offices. "Running a team and trying to win in this league is a full-time, year-long activity. It's hard enough to do it when all of your attention is only on football. And that's what I'm into—football. But the focus put on the game by the media has brought so many externals in that it gets increasingly difficult to keep everybody's attention on football."

Like everyone else, Noll has his share of human foibles—more than most people, some would say—but hypocrisy is not one of them. He remains the only coach who does not want his own TV show, rejecting the idea on principle. A coach's show is a perk that fills the pocket while it massages the ego. I asked Noll why he didn't have one. He glared, "I'm a football coach." Yes, Chuck Noll glares answers.

Gordon and Dan Edwards, the current publicity director, have their hands full getting Chuck to go along with some of the media's needs. Gordon has said, "Chuck's basic problem is that he really doesn't understand these people's jobs. But he's gotten much better about going along with things." Up to a point, and that is the point at which he thinks going along can hurt his football team.

Chuck Noll does not suffer fools gladly at any time, but apparently he has really made an effort to get along better in recent years. "You should have seen Chuck in the seventies, when the team was beating everybody," recalls Dave Ailes of the *Greensburg Tribune Review*. "You'd ask about the performance of a player you thought played outstanding. He'd say, 'Yes, he handled his assignments relatively well.' He was insufferable. Hard times seem to have mellowed him just a tad."

Of course, if you caught Noll at the right time with the right question, you'd end up with something memorable. As when someone asked him in the early eighties why Sidney Thornton, a stone-handed fullback, fumbled so much. Noll replied, after a thoughtful pause, "Sidney has many problems, and they are great." Laughter. Then Noll added, "What do they do in Iran?" and made a chopping motion across his wrist. Much laughter.

One of the reasons the open-door policy works in Pittsburgh is its size as a media market—eighteenth nationally and slipping. The city is isolated and overlooked, which probably accounts for its being such a livable place for those human beings who refuse to follow the great solar migration. It is a comfortable haven from the big, the fast, the shoddy. In modern media terms, Pittsburgh is a small town.

There's enough competition among the body of football reporters to make them hustle for stories, but not so much to pressure them into missing the call wantonly. There's another corrective as well. Football matters here. People are savvy about their game: Gossip, innuendo, and cheap shots make intriguing reading, sure, but they won't take a journalist as far here as they would in some of the gaudier markets. When it comes to football coverage, Pittsburgh is a throwback to the days when most journalists were still ethically bound to try to get the call right.

You'd be hard pressed to get Chuck Noll to agree. When I interviewed him for my Malone story in 1986, I asked him how he felt about the rising criticism of his coaching. He said, while looking down at his widespread fingers on the table, "Most of the people who cover this team are lampreys." I expected more, but that was all.

My mind raced: *Lampreys, lampreys? What's a goddamned lamprey?* Noll can be intimidating in his erudition. He knows wines, he's learned scuba diving and underwater photography, he has his pilot's license and has flown his own plane. I didn't ask him what a lamprey was.

A lamprey, the dictionary explains, is "an eel-like cyclostome with a funnel-shaped, jawless, sucking mouth surrounded by rasping teeth with which it bores into the flesh of other fishes to suck their blood."

I didn't see the beat writers and the radio and TV guys as lampreys at all. Whatever they were, by conventional media standards their bites weren't particularly dangerous unless you happened to be unusually thin-skinned. Many of them thought that was precisely Chuck Noll's problem.

As I came to know the core of men who covered the Steelers, I could identify only one or two lampreys among them. No, if you were going to characterize them with a metaphor from nature, you'd have to see them as a flock or a herd or perhaps a swarm, bursting into the Steelers' locker room after a game and nudging and crowding players' cubicles, gathering at the Pittsburgh airport to board the team plane for away games, piling into Noll's weekly press conference and then darting off to look for team officials, assistant coaches, or players who might drop tidbits for a story. *Scavenging* isn't too exaggerated a description.

Bees crossed my mind—the bothersome rather than the killer variety. But even that was too strong. Then it hit me. *Flies*. That was it. Buzzing, flitting, swarming flies. They annoyed. And there was just enough gad in them to keep everyone off balance and relatively honest. They were irritating, yes, but not so intrusive or obnoxious that coaches and players couldn't get their jobs done.

No individual, no team, no organization, no institution should be so powerful or so insulated it doesn't have to brush flies out of its face from time to time. That is one of the functions of the press. And the Flies were always flitting about the Steelers, observing, listening, buzzing.

Of the approximately two dozen journalists on the Steelers beat, about half have joined since the team won its last Super Bowl. They seem to have been reasonably well accepted, albeit grudgingly, by the old guard, though the veterans never let the younger guys forget the decade they missed. Most of the old-timers' football conversations begin with "Jack Lambert used to . . ." or "Fats Holmes would . . ." Although they try to fight the impulse in their work, some of the old-timers can't help being critical of anything that doesn't measure up to the old Stillers and the old days. With these new Steelers, nothing compares favorably.

The least of the Flies are actually the most visible, the TV sportscasters for Pittsburgh's three network affiliates: Sam Nover, WPXI-TV (NBC), Stan Savran, WTAE-TV (ABC), and John Stiegerwald, KDKA-TV2 (CBS). They can't walk to the press entrance of Three Rivers from the parking lot on game day without fans calling out their names or stopping them for autographs. They aren't just reporters, they're personalities, faces we've had in the house. The print guys, who labor, like most linemen, in perfect public anonymity, can't help being a little jealous, but they are men of the world and understand its arbitrary inequalities.

Pittsburgh is still a two-newspaper town, a surprising fact in the face of its decreasing population. The morning *Post-Gazette* and afternoon *Press* are in sufficient competition to pressure their beat men to hustle for stories on the Steelers. Ed Bouchette ("It rhymes," he says; "Bouchette of the *Gazette,* can't forget") and Steve Hubbard for the *Press,* the main beat reporters, don't miss very much that goes on around the team. Their styles are very different: Bouchette, deceptively low-key, with an "Oh, you don't say" approach; Hubbard more the accusative "Where were you supposed to have been on that play?" sort. Bouchette seems to do a little better. The old expression is true: Flies get more Steelers with sugar than with vinegar.

The soul of the swarm is a composite group, the writers from the small papers in the towns surrounding Pittsburgh, where faith in football and the Stillers constitutes a foundation of belief in life. Vic Ketchman is the sports editor of the *Standard Observer.* Dave Ailes does the same job for the *Greensburg Tribune Review.* Mike Prisuta writes for the *Beaver County Times.* Then there's Jim Kriek, the *Uniontown Herald-Standard;* Ron Musselman, the *Valley News Dispatch;* Tom Rose, the *Washington Observer Reporter;* Al King, the *Indiana Gazette;* Sam Ross, the *Johnstown Tribune Democrat;* Norm Vargo, the *McKeesport Daily News.*

These men are the true football press. They sit in frigid, wooden press boxes, covering high school games on Friday night, writing stories into the early morning for Saturday's paper. On Saturday afternoon it's usually small-college football, unless they're on the road with the Steelers, in which case they've boarded the team charter on Saturday morning. When the Steelers are home, the newsmen are up in the Three Rivers press box on Sundays. Throughout the league as well as in the visiting team's locker room at Three Rivers, they run into NFL players they've first covered all the way back in high school.

"It's important," says Ketchman, the purest of the purists, "not to forget where we came from, what the game means, and what we owe it in our work." There are enough Flies with this rare level of professionalism that the Steelers really never need worry about an all-out lamprey attack.

"Not many teams would take writers from papers with such small circulations on the road," Joe Gordon brags. "But this business isn't just a numbers game. You have to consider how loyal the fans these guys write for have been to us over the years. We owe them a lot." Then Gordon's normally large eyes grow immense. "It makes good sense from a marketing point of view also."

There are a variety of financial arrangements between the organizations the Flies represent and the Steelers. In some instances, the team picks up the tabs for the flight and the hotel room; in others, the Flies, who have made their own way to the game site, hop on the team charter back to Pittsburgh because it's so convenient. And there are Flies who make it a point to accept almost nothing from the Steelers because it could compromise their objectivity about the team. But even these few, when questioned closely, have not remained absolutely pure.

It is virtually impossible to do so. If the paper or station insists on reimbursing the Steelers for the seat on the charter, does it also pick up the tab for the extra beer, the chocolate bars for the kids, the

T-shirts, the autographed photos and footballs? And what about those free lunch spreads before the ball game and at Noll's Monday press conference?

Maybe the Steelers take along more writers from the smaller papers than some other teams, and maybe they pick up more of the bills, but to some degree most NFL teams make the same arrangements, especially in cities from the nonmajor markets. It's a system the big-name writers say is dead, that went out when journalism started taking itself seriously. It isn't, and it lives unhypocritically in Pittsburgh.

Interestingly, it does not automatically follow that because a Fly lets the Steelers take him to a football game, he'll jump right into their pocket. I paid close attention to the coverage of the '88 season and discovered that integrity was, as ever, a private and personal matter, not necessarily associated with accepting perks. Some of the toughest critics were letting the team pay a lot of the bills, while some of the pussy cats had the greatest financial independence. The level of journalistic objectivity overall, however, was what it was in most other cities; more important, it was about what it should have been.

Cope was always critical of football decisions that didn't make sense to him: Well into the season he was still raking Noll's fourth-down-run call against Dallas in Game One. Ed Bouchette, in his own modest fashion, regularly dug up tough stories on who was screwing up and how they did it. When the Steelers had punting problems, Bouchette discovered who blew assignments. He stayed on the Merriweather case all season.

Vic Ketchman was forthright in identifying Steelers who just couldn't cut it; his particular target was a scouting staff that wasn't finding the quality players this team needed. Marvin "Goose" Goslin, a KDKA radio sportscaster, warned his listeners early in the season, as he had in recent years, not to expect too much, and later he attacked the coaching staff for not doing enough to develop the young talent that was there.

Even Bob Labriola, a former Fly for the *Greensburg Tribune Review* who had been hired by Dan Rooney to edit the *Steelers Digest,* maintained a remarkable honesty for an in-house man. "How the hell am I going to write this one up?" he'd moan when an odious Steelers performance began smelling up Three Rivers. But he wrote the honest stink into his stories.

The strongest force in keeping most of them objective most of the time was their commitment to the game and to a readership and an audience that knew and loved the game as well as, and probably better than, its counterpart anywhere else in America. These fans would see through deception in a minute. Not only did they keep the football media in Pittsburgh relatively clean, they kept them reporting and writing about the game at the highest level.

Most of the Flies were from Pittsburgh, liked the town, and wanted the Steelers to do well. But they got the call right most of the time. Like many other things in this town, it's a purity of feeling connected somehow to the Spirit of Place.

Some of the TV people do not sense the Spirit in quite the same way. The majority of the writers felt they "made it" when they got jobs covering the Stillers—their boyhood dreams had been fulfilled. By nature, TV types seem impelled to move, or at least to look, ever onward and upward, to bigger and still bigger markets, to national prominence. It's the business. The main difference between print and TV is, for one thing, size of appetite.

Ketchman perceives another difference too. He sees it as "substance versus style, and the print guys are the substance." Maybe he's right: Guys who work for papers are called writers; the TV guys are called "talents."

The players understand this distinction. When Sam Nover does his TV show from the locker room after a home game, the players seem to like going on. It is almost a continuation of the game, just a little closer and more personal. Often they'll still be in pads or heavily taped, the gladiator direct from the arena. Occasionally, they'll be naked from the waist down, but the audience won't get to see that. They'll be on only a minute or two, and Nover will just have time to ask a couple of general things. The players get to control what the audience hears.

When they walk back to their cubicles, a dozen writers will be hovering with notebooks opened, pencils poised. The questions will come pretty fast, they'll be more specific, and there'll be follow-ups. It won't be very easy for the players to shape the result or even control the context. No Steeler I talked to, not even Tunch the accommodating, said he actually enjoyed talking to the press.

Embarkation on Saturday morning for a Steelers road game is like a roundup of sleepy strays. Players and media people begin to saunter woozily into Greater Pittsburgh International Airport more than an hour before Noll's declared time. Mike Webster, whose fifteen excellent seasons have skewed the league's longevity average, is usually first on the scene. He is a prudent, precise professional, and a worrier. Other large men drift into the circular waiting area, moving slowly, acting exactly as they are dressed—quietly casual. Noll does not believe in telling grown men what they should wear. He is not the black-blazer-with-gold-team-insignia type.

Out on Route 60, some of the oversleepers are speeding to the airport while scanning their rearview mirrors for cops. If they do get pulled over, they'll probably end up with a police escort. All the players carry playbooks and game plans; some of the early birds opt to do a little studying while waiting to board. They hope the coaches are watching.

It's easy to distinguish the Flies. Much smaller and older, of course, they are a pretty unhealthy lot even compared to the general population. There are more than a few smokers among them. They arrive both early and late.

Vic Ketchman has a cigarette hanging from his lips as he moves stiffly toward the waiting area, a suit bag slung over his shoulder. He looks dreadful, and he knows it. He explains, "I covered a high school game last night. Freezing press box. Real bad game too. Tough story to write. But eventually I wrote something decent. I didn't get to bed until almost five."

"Just for a high school game?"

His eyes flash. "Greensburg High School, the Pittsburgh Steelers, no difference; these people want good, accurate reporting."

It's all football and this is western Pennsylvania.

There is an inflexible seating arrangement on the plane that reflects the team's pecking order. Steelers team officials and coaches populate the posh first-class section. The players occupy the regular seating section, filling from the front to about two thirds of the way back, leaving an empty seat between window and aisle on each side to accommodate their bulk. Flies fill the rear. They may or may not have the convenience of an open seat depending on how many of them are making the trip. When Dan Edwards, the PR man, calls, "Triple up, guys," the Flies buzz and bitch until they realize they have no choice but to close ranks.

Coaches occasionally drift back and talk to some of the players. Otherwise, fraternization among the groups is by invitation only. And invitations are rarely offered. Most of the players are still looking at their playbooks or sleeping or thinking about the game, their careers, or this strange, pressurized way they are making a living. The veteran flight crew has worked these Steelers flights for years, and they're familiar and efficient. The food is many cuts above ordinary airline fare in both quantity and quality: shrimp cocktail, crabmeat, grilled steaks, large salads, juice, ice cream, cake, and pie. Seconds are available. One meal would feed five on a regularly scheduled flight.

The plane carries a heavy load, and not only because most of the men on it are huge. Although everyone brings rather minimal carry-ons, more than two tons of football and supporting equipment go into the cargo hold of the plane before anyone boards. It will be off-loaded and trucked to the stadium while the players disembark.

While they have all flown a great many times in their lives, very few of the players are completely comfortable in the air. Steve Bono, the third-string quarterback, leans over to Dermontti Dawson and Mike Hinnant, a pair of rookie linemen, and says with mock confidence, "Nothing to worry about, guys, there's never been a professional team that's crashed yet." A Fly behind Bono hears and corrects, "Not over the continental United States, anyway."

Depending on how long the flight lasts, a raucous card game called Boo-Ray breaks out early or late in the very rear of the plane. The Boo-Ray regulars are team trainer Ralph Berlin, orthopedist Dr. Tom Cowan, Dan Ferens, the office manager, and Jim "Buff" Boston, who is listed in the Steelers' media guide as "Chief Negotiator" but whose exact duties vary with the situation, a troubleshooter/jack-of-all-trades type. On the road, for example, Buff is responsible for the transfer of equipment, and so far if the Steelers have arrived, so has their stuff.

Apparently Boo-Ray is humiliating and expensive to losers, exciting to everyone, because the Boo-Rayers always make lots of noise and are constantly seeking new suckers. The game is a strange combination of poker and pinochle with a $5 ante and a starting pot of $30 that keeps doubling when a player doesn't take a trick. Watching players drawing cards and playing trumps gives a bystander the impression that they're making up the game as they go along. I wanted to give it a shot but didn't dare.

Choice seats near the rear are set aside for Joe Gordon, Dan

Edwards, and Pat Hanlon, Dan's assistant. The last window seat on the left-hand side of the plane had been John Stallworth's until he retired in 1987. This year Bubby Brister has chosen it. "I don't know why, exactly. Stallworth always looked comfortable back here. Isn't the tail of the plane safer than the front?" The seat is seven or eight rows behind the players' section and just about as far from Chuck Noll's seat as Bubby can get. He sleeps much of the time on the plane, or pretends to.

The window seat directly in front of the one Bubby has inherited from Stallworth has long been claimed by Myron Cope. For anyone from Pittsburgh that name requires no further explanation. For those who are not from Pittsburgh, how in the world do I begin to introduce Myron Cope?

I begin, I guess, by saying that Myron is, first and foremost, a voice, an utterly unique and unforgettable Pittsburgh voice. Myron's talk show, *Cope on Sports,* is as Pittsburgh as an "Imp and an Iron." With Myron, though, it's not so much what he says—and no one around is any more knowledgeable—it's how he says it.

Imagine the broadest local dialect possible, but one that treats vowel sounds as though they tasted bad. Add an adenoidal twang as abrasive as a zipper being forced open. Give an element of suspenseful surprise to each articulated word, as though it didn't know itself if it might still become a question. Sprinkle all the above with cadences not generally heard around Pittsburgh since the first immigrant children learned English. Top this off with exclamations of "Hoo-hah" or staccato Yiddish, and you've got Myron Cope on the air.

Cope first gave radio a shot in 1968, when the station manager at WTAE told him, "We see a trend toward obnoxious voices." Since 1970, Cope's also been doing color commentary and analysis on Steelers games, working with Jack Fleming, one of the smoothest, most relaxed play-by-play men in the business. Putting this odd couple of voices together was a touch of genius.

Even if you hate sports, you can't escape Myron in Pittsburgh. He'll get you with one of his ubiquitous radio or TV commercials when you least expect it. (A joke among the Flies is that Myron never met a commercial he didn't like.) Most of the time, Myron leaves 'em laughing. There are those, however, who react as though they're hearing fingernails on a blackboard. Myron is not an acquired taste: You'll know instantly if you can stand him. In Pittsburgh, Myron suits an awful lot of people.

Viewers who finally get to see a familiar radio voice on TV are usually surprised by how different he looks from what they expected. In Myron's case, the surprise is how much he looks like the voice, and how you feel you've always known him. Myron is a pixie—the twinkling eye, close-cropped curly hair, even one gnarled, slightly pointed ear. All in all, a leprechaun with chutzpah.

Cope's voice is exaggerated on the air, but only slightly. He really does speak that way, even though it is also his shtick. "Hel-low, yer on the air with Myron Cope," he'll say to a typical caller to his talk show, making the *o* in his name sound like a three-vowel diphthong.

"Hey, Maa-ron. I was at the ballpark fer the opener, and we were sure lucky as hell. What d'you think?"

"There was, I would have to say, an element of good fortune in our victory—yes, we were smiled upon. But I also thought we played good enough to win. Listen, yer going to lose enough of those kinds of games over the course of a season, so why not be happy when you win it?"

"Know what rilly got to me, Maa-ron? I wanted a hot dog and when I got to the counter I saw a sign said twenty-five cents extra for sauerkraut. Maa-ron, do you think it's fair I should have to pay extra for *kapusta*?" (It's the Polish equivalent.)

"So don't have it with *kapusta* if you're a cheapskate. Or bring

your own *kapusta*. I don't care what you do with your *kapusta*—
we're here to talk Stillers."

Cope grew up in Squirrel Hill and went to the University of
Pittsburgh on a baseball scholarship. His number two dream, when
it became clear he wasn't going to play second base for the Pirates,
was to become a Pittsburgh newspaper man, and after serving an
apprenticeship at the *Erie Times,* he was hired by the *Post-Gazette*
in 1952.

Cope left the paper eight years later to free-lance for magazines,
a daring move for any writer, but one that reflected his strong
self-confidence. Cope was a superb feature writer, contributing regularly to *Life, Look, The Saturday Evening Post, Time,* and *Sports
Illustrated*. He didn't have to hustle too hard for work; mostly, it
came to him because Cope was good and the New York editors knew
it. His specialty was eccentric athletes. "I became known in the
business as a writer of flakes—or maybe as a flaky writer, however
you want it."

Cope smokes heavily, and on the plane his smoke drifts right back
to Bubby and everyone else in the vicinity. Bubby doesn't complain.
Nobody does. Among all the journalists who travel with the Steelers,
Myron Cope has earned patriarchal status. He is the silently ac-
knowledged, tiny, benevolent Lord of the Flies.

If the plane has left early on a Saturday morning, Noll will not
have had his team practice at Three Rivers, so usually the players
will be bused to the stadium so they can get a feel for the terrain
and walk through key elements of the game plan one more time.
When the practice is over, most of the players will go back to the
hotel and watch college football on TV. Depending on their responsibilities, they also study the game plan to varying degrees. There are
always some who have relatives and old friends in town. And a great
many of these friends turn out to be beautiful young women.

Whenever the Steelers arrive in an NFL town, Dan Edwards

invites some of the Flies out to dinner. The restaurant of choice, usually one of the best in town, has come highly recommended, most often by the home team's PR man. The evening's objective is memorable eating, drinking, and talking. I was flattered with an invitation to join the select group just before midseason, but didn't accept for the most practical of reasons—I wasn't sure I could afford it. Later in the year, when I felt I could, I discovered one of the highlights of the Steelers' pregame rituals.

Seated prominently in fancy restaurants all around the league, a dozen or so Pittsburgh scribes stage a sporting Steeltown version of the old Algonquin round table, with Cope sitting in for Alexander Woollcott.

Pat Hanlon, who's a natural, unmitigated tease, might get things off to a rousing start by saying, "This game they play nowadays ain't really football, 'least not like it used to be in the old league, right, Myron?"

"Oh, no," says Norm Vargo, "don't get him going on the old Steelers. We've all heard about how they used to hang out at Dante's and drink until closing, and after closing, and then go out and play the next morning. We've heard all those stories."

Hanlon: "These guys are just a bunch of businessmen in football suits, right, Myron?" Myron doesn't look as though he's going to jump at the bait, so Hanlon adds, "Guys a lot more colorful in those days, right, Myron? Hell, even the women were tougher."

Myron can't resist. He says, very seriously, "That's one of the major problems with the game these days. These guys are so valuable to themselves, they don't want to give the body the way players used to. And you just can't play football right if you don't want to give the body." Then there's a mysterious segue no one understands but everyone accepts. "You should have seen the town after the war. There were places that never closed, and they offered every conceivable sort of temptation for the palate and for all the other senses as well. Why, there was one light-skinned black gal who was legendary in Pittsburgh. She cost a hundred bucks a night, which is like a thousand bucks these days, maybe more. Well, one night, I stopped in a little tavern on my way home . . ." Myron's tale builds slowly, gathering in famous baseball and football players, notorious gangsters, the gorgeous trollope, with Myron somehow driving a car full of these characters headed for a motel on the outskirts of town.

From this wonderful mishmash, Myron weaves a remarkable tapestry—especially when describing the temptress's *kapusta*—that ends not at the motel, but somehow back in the broadcast booth at Three Rivers, with Myron describing a play in the previous week's game that shows definitively why today's players aren't as great as their predecessors in the old league. The tale, understandably, has raised the eyebrows of most diners in the vicinity.

As the evening wears on, Myron doesn't have to be baited; he happily tells tales of the beasts and the flakes, the prodigious eaters, drinkers, and womanizers on the old Steelers. They were giants in those days. And, yes, old Art Rooney gets remembered frequently and fondly. Most of these tales have been heard before by the men around this table; no matter, the ritual retelling is the thing.

Inevitably, arguments break out over the worth of a Steelers player or a coach or a game strategy. It can get pretty loud. Except for the few diners who realize they're witnessing impassioned oral history of high quality, obvious discomfort registers on nearby faces. Only the participants are sorry when it is time to see the round table adjourned. When the check comes, Dan Edwards picks it up on behalf of the Steelers. We lift our glasses high.

The stars of sports print, in Pittsburgh as elsewhere, are the columnists: Gene Collier and Bob Smizik of the *Press,* Bruce Keidan of the *Post-Gazette*. Their pictures over their columns confirm that status. In their business, it isn't really important if they get the call

right; all they have to do is be entertaining as hell. And they are.
Each is in his own way a virtuoso performer who has the latitude to
choose event, point of view, and style (usually tantalizingly smug).
On Sundays during football season, they do the Steelers.

Talk to Steelers players about the writers who bother them most
and it's frequently the columnists who crop up. Talk a little more,
and you discover that many players don't really know the difference
between a news story and a column. "Don't whatever they print in
the paper have to be true?" Earnest Jackson, the much-traveled
fullback, asked before he stopped talking to the media. I attempted
to explain the difference between a reporter and a columnist, and
when I finished he said, "Then that must put columns in the same
category as science-fiction movies." By George, he's got it.

Tunch Ilkin's bête noire is Bruce Keidan. "I see him slinking
around the locker room with his notebook and I think, 'How's he
going to hurt this team now?' Then I see him coming over here and
I know I've really got to be on my guard."

My own informal poll around the Steelers' locker room and offices
revealed that Keidan is indeed the columnist most people would
prefer to see slinking the other way. I ended up joining that group
when this book became Keidan's subject. I picked up a *Post-Gazette*
one morning after the Steelers looked particularly inept, in fact their
least ept of the season. Under the head IS IT TIME TO CLOSE THE
BOOK ON NOLL?, I saw this Keidan lead: "Sam Toperoff is writing a
book about the 1988 Steelers. Poor Sam. Random House gave him
an advance, and he spent it. It is too late to turn back now." I had
been Keidan-ed.

What the column did was link me and my project to Noll's utter
failure as a coach. With this kind of "creativity," there is nothing
a clever cynic or troublemaker can't do in print. No wonder the
players cringe when some of these guys saunter over. Still, even this
wasn't a full-fledged lamprey attack, not if you're familiar with what

Dick Young used to pull up in New York. I nicknamed Keidan "Tighten-the-Noose Bruce" and carried on. I hadn't spent the advance either.

Noll, because he was so aloof and contentious during his great winning years, had become, in defeat, too delectable a target for the press. Some critics called Noll the "Pope," not because he was the vicar of the church of the last dynasty but because his haughtiness gave the impression he was always out on a balcony looking down on the common folk. There was an air of papal infallibility about him too, at least while talking football to the unwashed. And he had a way of making everyone feel unwashed.

It is understatement to say Chuck Noll is a very complicated man. He does not respect the media, yet he has learned to accommodate it well enough over the years. Of course, he rarely gives away anything he doesn't want them to have. He is fiercely proud of his knowledge, not just of football but of all sorts of other fields as well; as a result, he comes across as cold and pedantic. Yet he manages to hold the respect of most of his players on the emotional gut level of the playing field.

He is accused of having a rigid, predictable football philosophy, yet was flexible enough to do the unexpected when defenses began to read his mind; and he was very good at position adjustments when his player resources were depleted by injury. Chuck Noll is a man, who, given his choice, would labor in complete anonymity, and to all but those in his inner circle, he is a perfect enigma. Even to some of the men in the front office, he remains a partial enigma, which is, when you think about it, even tougher to figure out.

Now, with the Steelers and Chuck Noll losing, and losing often, it was just too good a story to pass up for some of the Flies he had patronized in his successful days. A proud, even an arrogant man humbled. Just too good to pass up.

Noll, of course, refused to show any signs of cracking and never deigned to respond to media criticism. There were no public breast-beatings, never an emotional *mea culpa*. Privately, he did admit to error: According to Tony Dungy, Noll told his staff just before midseason that he had overestimated the players' abilities and had asked them to do things they were not capable of.

For the team, it was actually a pretty good thing Noll was such an irresistible high-profile target; he became a lightning rod for criticism, so most of the others were spared the brunt of it.

Mean Joe Greene always read most of what was written about the teams he played on and coached for. Even when those stories got the call right, he believed they focused on the wrong things. A story either overwhelmed the reader with statistics, or got too gossipy, too far from the field. The real story, according to Joe (who really ought to be renicknamed "Wise" Joe Greene), took place between the lines, the sidelines. "Gentlemen, you don't understand," he told a group of Flies once. "There are a lot of honest-to-God human confrontations going on out there." Wise Joe's journalism lesson ought to be inscribed in press boxes throughout the league.

Football is raw human drama, and it bothered Joe then, and bothers him still, that football's truest stories don't get told often enough. Frankie Pollard, the running back, once told me, "There's got to come a time when I won't be standing in a huddle. I'll miss the breathing, the looks in guys' eyes, the trying to be calm in the nervousness. That's a part of football no one knows."

ONE STEP TOO MANY,
ONE PASS TOO SHORT

There is no secret about how to win consistently in the NFL: Put together good, compatible talent (you don't have to be awesome up and down the roster, though of course that wouldn't hurt); make the players believe they're good enough to win against players as good as they are; then go out on the playing field on Sunday and do what you believe you are good enough to do; once those difficult tasks are accomplished, you then try the impossible—doing it every single Sunday.

All the steps are tough, but that last one seems the toughest. "They've got to learn how to win" is the expression you hear around the league applied to all the teams with some talent that haven't yet crossed that invisible borderline into excellence. It's an expression coaches and veteran players find hard to break down to specifics except by pointing to the teams that have done it. Cincinnati and Minnesota did it in 1988, and Philadelphia seems on the verge.

At the very least, it means having most of your players doing the right things most of the time and especially in crucial game situations. According to Tony Dungy, "The upper-echelon teams in the league seem to have the ability to make big plays when they're needed. They usually have superior concentration on defense; they make you beat them with big plays—they refuse to beat themselves. I see it as a combination of desire, experience, and intelligence."

Experience can come only with time, but it is also a matter of how players respond to crunch situations, which makes certain players grow up a little faster. Losing the hard way seems to be a necessary precondition of "learning how to win," but it's something Noll despises. He told a Fly who was an unbridled Steelers optimist, "It's true, there are important lessons to be learned from adversity, but nothing, *nothing* teaches ultimate success better than winning does." You might say Chuck Noll thinks losing is extremely overrated.

Joe Greene doesn't want to hear about the ultimate value of adversity either. In 1969, Greene's first year with the Steelers, the team won their first game. "I thought, 'This league ain't that tough.'" The Steelers went on to lose their next thirteen. "If we were learning how to win then, no one bothered to tell me about it. By the tenth week I wanted to go home. It was so bad, I lost the entire month of November."

The venerable Arthur McEnery saw all those games, and he recalls, "Even watching the old Forbes Field Steelers lose wasn't particularly unpleasant, but seeing that team lose was painful, maybe because one sensed there were some talented men here who were being humiliated week after week."

For the very inexperienced '88 Steelers, the Redskins game was critical. Washington was one of the most talented, accomplished teams in the league and therefore heavily favored. If the Steelers played well, it would be a giant step toward getting this young group, who didn't really know what to think about themselves and were searching for their identity, to believe they could be a decent football team. If they got blown away, no one knew what the psychological fallout could be. In professional football, only success can bring conviction, and sometimes even that isn't enough.

It was just the second game of the season, but everyone from Dan Rooney to Tony Parisi, the equipment manager, knew how important this game was. Rooney said, "I won't say we'll win, but I believe we'll be able to play with this team. We'll have to overcome nerves and inexperience and the Redskins and a hostile crowd, but I truly believe we can do it. Why shouldn't we win? Someone has to, so why not the boys from Pittsburgh?" Why not, indeed.

On the bus to RFK Stadium players stare stonily at the D.C. motorcycle cops cutting a swatch for the buses through the parkway traffic. They've got such a tight hold on their emotions, the tension in the air is thick and palpable.

The Steelers lead at the half 13–10 on a career-building pass by Brister to Louis Lipps. While Brister drops straight back, looks left, and pumps, Lipps streaks down the right sideline. All-Pro corner Darrell Green has bitten on the Brister pump fake and is a corpse. The perfectly thrown pass deep down the sideline is the least of Brister's achievement. There are some quarterbacks in the NFL who will never be able to freeze a cornerback that well. It is hard to believe this is only Brister's fourth game as a starter.

As is common in the NFL, the game is on the line in the second half. It will actually turn on a single play in the third quarter. After the Steelers have opened a nine-point lead, the Redskins have the ball on their own 30, third down and a yard to go. They bring on extra tight ends for what should be a short-yardage running play to maintain possession. The Steelers pack in their defense to jam the run. Doug Williams, the Super Bowl MVP, fakes his fullback on a dive into the line, but, hiding the ball on his hip, loops back, turns, and throws to his reserve tight end, who has slipped behind Steelers corner Rod Woodson. Woodson, assuming the run, has taken one step too far back toward the line of scrimmage.

A magnificent athlete starting only his second game at cornerback, Woodson is a confident sort who believes there's nothing he can't do on a football field. He has the potential to be a great player—someday. Today, however, Doug Williams teaches him a painful lesson as a nine-point lead is suddenly reduced to two. The hope is Woodson has learned something about the NFL, but at quite a cost.

Nevertheless, the Steelers get the touchdown back and are ahead by 29–20 with about nine minutes left in the game. I'm convinced they are going to defeat the Super Bowl champs on their own field. I don't quite know how they've done it, but I'm excited for them and for myself. In my notebook I jot, very unprofessionally since they haven't yet won the game, "Beating the Super Bowl champs! What a year to follow the Steelers. This win makes my book."

No sooner have I written those words than Doug Williams starts to drive the Skins the length of the field, and it's 29–27. There are less than five minutes left, and if the Steelers can maintain possession and run some clock, they can hold on. But they go three downs and out and have to give the ball back almost immediately. Then the Skins' superior size and execution finally tips the balance. The Steelers' defense has almost nothing left. Washington controls the ball, the field, and the clock. A short Washington field goal with fourteen seconds left wins 30–29. The difference, by the way, was a missed Steelers' extra point on the reliable Mike Webster's bad snap.

For the Steelers, it's a withering loss.

In the locker room afterward everyone is hurting. Dan Rooney walks slump-shouldered as though he's taken a body blow. Joe Gordon is glassy-eyed, but asserts, "I saw losses just like this one in the early seventies. After that we were gangbusters." Except for a fumble lost by Earnest Jackson, there were no turnovers.

A Fly asks Noll, "You didn't have a very good defensive game and still almost won—what does that mean to you?"

Noll glares. "It means we didn't have a very good defensive game and still almost won." The end of the statement is not the end of the glare.

Mike Webster prides himself in his ability to cope, to handle the great successes and the rare bitter defeats with equanimity. Now he must talk about his misdirected extra-point snap that cost a ball game. His voice is tempered but his eyes are glazed: "There's no excuse for that. It's just disgusting. I've been doing it for fifteen years. You just can't make that mistake. It's got to be automatic. You've got to make it every time, not nine out of ten or ninety-nine out of a hundred, but every single time."

While he pulls a brush through his damp hair, Bubby is saying, "What do I think this team needs? I only know what I need. And right now, I need a beer real bad. Matter of fact, I think I'll meet Myron tonight over at the Holiday Inn for a few."

When the quiet linebacker David Little can finally talk about it, he says, "If this team needed proof it had talent and character, playing these guys, the champs, to a standstill ought to prove that." It sounds true enough, but for all the brave and inspiring talk, this is a business where only results ultimately matter. When people look at the team standings in the newspaper, the Steelers have won one and lost one. And that's all.

No one knows for sure how the players will respond, but there is one very bad sign. Jackson tells the Flies his fumble was Brister's fault, claiming the handoff was poor. It is a point of honor on truly professional teams like Noll's not to blame someone else for an error. And never, never with a Fly around to hear it. Brister tries to defuse a lousy situation by saying about the fumble, "Sure, I'll take the blame on that one." Bubby knows when he says it, as films will later confirm, that there was nothing wrong with the handoff. Still, Steve Hubbard's sidebar about the fumble in the *Press* is provocatively headed, WHO IS TO BLAME? There are players in the Steelers' locker room who will no longer speak to Hubbard.

GAME DAY 3: SUNDAY, SEPTEMBER 18

Cincinnati (2-0) at Pittsburgh (1-1)

"Well, Frank, what'd you think about last week?"

Krupka, who knows he might get quoted, is thoughtful. "The boys played real good. Don't know if they can play any better than that. But still they lost. I wonder what it'll do to their spirit."

Nothing has changed but the color of my rented car. The lawn chairs are the same; the beer and burgers, the Blazer, number 75, the missus, everything the same, except this time it's cloudy. A Polish-language program is coming over a nearby portable radio.

"So what do you expect today?"

"Today could tell us all we need to know," Krupka says. "If they can recover from last week, fine. If not, it could be the end of their season."

The Steelers play an unsure, error-filled first half against their AFC Central rivals. The Bengals were the joke of the league during the '87 season, a team loaded with talent that ended up 4-11 and went from week to week finding new ways to lose. Yet, after a bundle of Steelers fumbles, an interception, and a host of sacks on Brister, the Steelers trail only 7–2 at halftime. To play this badly and not be blown away is a sign of hope at halftime in NFL locker rooms.

In the third quarter, John Rienstra, who has quietly been playing improving football every week since he returned to training camp, has the terrible luck of merely being in the vicinity when Earnest Jackson is tackled after a run downfield. Jackson is rolled into Rienstra, who goes down like he's shot. Instantly, Rienstra has a broken tibia. Misfortune follows John around like a repo man.

When a player is hurt, the other players are genuinely sympathetic, but the unspoken response is always a little more complicated. Injury is the scourge of life in the NFL, the grim reaper, so each player is secretly glad he isn't the one who's out of action, though he's certainly not proud of such feelings. Of course, he knows it could just as easily have been him. And for every player who goes down, a backup gets the chance to show what he can do, so someone else's misfortune can be another player's chance of a lifetime. The entire subject is so psychologically complicated that players learn to live with it by almost never acknowledging it.

Twice the Steelers push the ball inside the Cincinnati 10 with first downs, but neither time can they punch it in. "Learning how to win" means precisely this—learning how to score when you've got the opportunity. Nevertheless, after an Anderson field goal and with five minutes left in the game, the Steelers lead 12–10. If Krupka is right, here is their season. If they hold on to win, it will confirm the Washington loss as nothing more than a bad break. If they fold here, how in the world will they ever be able to believe in themselves?

There's barely time to think about any of these ramifications because Boomer Esiason throws 65 yards to a wide-open Eddie Brown for a 17–12 lead. On the play, Brown has beaten Delton Hall badly. Afterward, Noll will admit, "That was my fault. . . . Delton was playing with a groin injury, and we had him in a situation where he couldn't run."

It is in a final drive to win a game where character and confidence are forged, where NFL quarterbacks and teams are tested to the ultimate. Professionalism, thy name is the Two-Minute Drill.

Brister takes the ball with 1:54 left and directs his teammates to the Bengals' 20; there's plenty of time, a minute on the clock. The pivotal play: Running back Rodney Carter will slide out of the backfield and glide down the right sideline toward the end zone. The pass is going to take awhile to develop, so the protection must hold. Brister rolls slightly left and looks only at receivers on that side—hell, it worked against Washington last week, why not again?—then he turns back to the right. Carter is open near the end zone. Momentarily. It will take a long, diagonal throw.

Eric Thomas, the right cornerback, is zone-covering. Afterward, he will say, "I hung in on the seam and, when the ball was thrown, reacted to the outside." That isn't quite what I saw. I saw Thomas slip momentarily and get caught in the wrong spot, which turned out to be the right spot when he made his interception.

Brister says, "I saw Rodney flash open and I tried to drive him the ball. I guess the guy was leading me and broke toward the ball when I was throwing it. Maybe a split second sooner or a split second later I had Rodney for a TD." Or maybe a pass looped over Thomas's head. Next season, perhaps. "But it was a miserable pick [pickoff]." In Brister's drawl the word sounds like "pig," a better description.

At the time, no one could know how good a team the Steelers had lost to. The Bengals would end up in the Super Bowl, losing their lead to the 49ers with only thirty-four seconds left in the game.

Brister's evaluation of this game is terse and apt: "We were in the game somehow, and then the wheels came off."

At his press conference, Noll is asked if the defense misses Mike Merriweather. It's a loaded question likely to go off no matter how Noll responds, but he defuses it: "I'll only talk about players who want to be here."

The strongest specific criticism in the press seems to be directed at Delton Hall, even though he is playing hurt. Counting the final preseason game, he has now been beaten for six touchdowns in four games. But generally speaking the Flies have been reasonable. One explanation is that the two with the sharpest pens are elsewhere: Keidan of the *Post-Gazette* is in Korea covering the Olympics; Gene Collier of the *Press* is taking some time off because his wife is expecting a baby. But neither the Olympics nor the pregnancy will last forever.

7

TONY DUNGY IS
LOOKING FOR LEADERS

I'm supposed to meet Tony Dungy, the defensive coordinator, in his office. I don't know exactly where that is and drift instead through the corridor where I saw him last. At the end of the hallway I see a darkened conference room where three men are watching game films. I slip unseen into a seat in the rear.

On the screen, Jim Kelly, the Buffalo Bills' quarterback, takes his drop in slow time, then an even further drop. Huge New England Patriots linemen are lumbering, also in painfully delayed motion, toward Kelly, who floats a perfectly timed screen pass to his halfback. All motion freezes; the ball zips itself from the receiver's hands back to Kelly, and everyone double-times backward jerkily to his original stance. The play is rerun twice more.

I listen as the defensive coaches talk about what little signs give away the screen pass. Then linebacker coach Jed Hughes spots me and whispers to Dungy, who explains, gently but firmly, "I'm afraid no one's allowed back here. I'll be out in a few minutes." Joe Greene's baleful gaze is like a finger pointed in my chest. I leave.

Within hours after every NFL game, each team sends a video-tape—even though working terminology is still "film"—of its game to the next week's opponent. During the night, while millions of fans sleep distressed or contentedly, dozens of game tapes will have been processed, shipped across or around the continent by express plane, and delivered by van. They are reproduced, cut, edited, and then ready for the offensive, defensive, and special teams coaches when they arrive for work early Monday morning.

It's all astoundingly efficient. Hughes, Greene, and Dungy are doing exactly what their counterparts up in Buffalo are doing with the Steelers' loss to Cincinnati. The Buffalo coaches won't be as glum; they beat New England. All of them will look for hours, hoping to discover offensive patterns, tendencies, tip-offs that their defenses can exploit, maybe even attack, because defenses no longer just respond to offenses.

The defense might, for example, overload one side of the field or pack a particular gap in the line, ensuring that the play that has been called and the formation the offense is in is doomed before the ball is even snapped. So the offensive coordinator had better have installed a workable variation and the quarterback better be smart enough to switch to it when he sees the defense.

"You always try to look at the films with a fresh eye," Dungy explains later when he has a few minutes between chores, "hoping you'll spot a little giveaway somewhere. Maybe a quarterback will do something different when he's throwing deep or setting up the screen. Contrary to some of those stories you hear about how a coach in the screening room at two A.M. sees something that ends up winning a big game, you really don't find anything concrete very often. Mostly you just get a better sense of their newer personnel and their basic offensive philosophy. From that we'll formulate our defensive game plan."

Although Dungy is in charge of the defensive backs as well as being the coordinator, the setting of the weekly defensive tactics and strategy starts out as a collaborative effort. Greene and Hughes make judgments about what their units might be able to do against the Bills; Dungy does the same with his secondary. Because each group is dependent upon the other—even more than usual this season because Greene's down linemen aren't establishing a decent pass rush—there's a good deal of give-and-take. Greene's guys are doing more of the taking at this point, the linebackers and defensive backs the giving.

If the defense is going to show an opposing quarterback a number of different and potentially confusing "looks" (formations), each unit will have to make adjustments. The key player in that regard so far has been Aaron Jones. Because Jones is so swift for a big man (six feet, four and a half inches, 260 pounds), Hughes has suggested making him something of a "rover," lining him up on either side of the ball and back off the line of scrimmage with the linebackers. The Denver Broncos had great success doing the same thing with Karl Mecklenburg. Hughes had asked Greene about trying the experiment in training camp, and Joe said, "Let's try it and see how it goes. Don't want to confuse my young lion too much and ask him to do more than he can at this stage."

By assenting, Greene permitted Dungy to inject a great deal of variety into the defensive plan—the Steelers could go with three down linemen and four backers or quickly jump into a four-three adjustment at the last minute without changing personnel. Against Buffalo Aaron would line up at five different positions, once even covering a potential receiver coming out of the backfield. The wrinkle was intended to confuse Jim Kelly. As it turned out, it ended up confusing Aaron Jones, who hadn't yet mastered down-lineman requirements before being bounced around.

In similar fashion, the Steelers' defensive game plan evolves as Monday wears on, a collaboration among Greene, Hughes, and Dungy. "It's pretty much a series of compromises," says Dungy, "because, although we have a general sense of what we'd each like to try to do against a particular opponent, we also know what our individual limitations are. And we've got to make sure we each know the limitations of the other units, and [their] strengths, so that we cover for one another."

It is also important to try to determine an opponent's key injuries for an upcoming game. In most cases, there is no way to know on Monday or Tuesday if a certain injured player will be able to perform on Sunday, but as more information comes in, Dungy has to be prepared to exploit any weaknesses.

When there's enough agreement among the defensive staff, Tony Dungy literally coordinates; that is, he maps on paper an overall strategy that reflects each coach's judgment of strengths and needs. He'll list the opponent's general tendencies according to field position and down. He'll describe the most desirable defensive alignments for all likely situations, along with the personnel he wants on the field. And he'll be sure his secondary knows when to zone-cover if the occasion requires.

After he checks the plan out with Greene and Hughes, Dungy brings it to Noll. "Usually Chuck will go along with us. Once in a while he'll make a personnel change. He'll want to take a look at one guy over another. If he makes any strategy changes, he usually has a good reason," Dungy explains.

Tony Dungy works very hard—seventy and eighty hours a week during the season. Most of his time is spent watching game film, attending meetings, and demonstrating techniques on the practice field. It's concentrated, dedicated work but not the coaching madness you sometimes hear about: coaching staffs who sleep and eat at stadiums so they can be at the ready all week long, so every possible contingency will be covered.

What does happen is that those coaches will burn out in their early forties, like Dick Vermeil of the Eagles; their marriages will disintegrate at roughly the same time, and so will their health. But in a very impermanent business, such dedication at least shows the fans, the media, and, most of all, the boss that they're doing everything humanly—and inhumanly—possible to win. Whatever else they may be faulted for, the work ethic won't be an issue.

Noll believes in working hard and smart, but he also believes in family and a sense of perspective. "Chuck wants football to be number one, but he also wants his people to have a life away from football," Dungy says. "And it's a good thing. You can lose your effectiveness by overcommitting and trying *too* hard and losing your sense of what's important. There are nights I don't get home till ten P.M. but most of the time it's closer to eight or nine. At least I'll be fresh the next day and maybe with some perspective be able to rethink some problem we're having.

"There's great strain on a marriage in this business. Especially for a young coach trying to make his mark if he has little children. It's not only all the hours we put in and the long separations, it's also the problem of how different a coach's world is from his family's. There are some wives who don't know what their husbands really do and don't even want to know. I try to tell my wife what my problems are and she tries to understand. I try for quality time with my children, but during the season it's tough. Fortunately, Chuck understands what it's like to be a family man. I really appreciate that."

When Tony got home after the tough loss in Washington, he and Lauren talked about what had gone wrong. After the children went to sleep, Tony and Lauren took the dogs on a long walk through their suburban neighborhood, talking a little more about the Washington game; rather, Tony talked and Lauren listened and asked intelligent questions. The season would be full of such walks.

Dungy, whose grandfather was a minister, belongs to one of the team's weekly Bible-study groups. In fact, when he played on the Steelers, Tony was introduced to Lauren by the minister of his church. "The minister kept saying there was a girl I really ought to meet, but I kept putting it off. I thought, 'What kind of girl would a minister introduce me to?' But he persisted. It turned out she wasn't too excited about meeting me either. She didn't think athletes were very reliable types. It didn't seem very promising." The Dungys have two small children.

Tony Dungy grew up in Jackson, Michigan, an automobile town near Detroit. His parents were people of remarkable accomplishment by any standards, but nothing short of extraordinary in Jackson's black and often economically depressed community. Tony's father has a Ph.D. in biology, and his mother is a schoolteacher with a master's degree. They made absolutely certain their children would not be swallowed by the socioeconomic pitfalls that brought down so many other kids in town. They succeeded. Tony's brother is a dentist, one of his sisters an obstetrician.

"It was a house with lots of books around, and not a single ashtray," Tony recalls. "Academics always came first. After that there was a place for sports. My mom was the athlete. She was from Windsor, Ontario, and played on the Canadian national basketball team."

Just in case his parents' positive values weren't strong enough, they were reinforced by a negative one. "My oldest sister married when she was eighteen. Her husband worked scraping tires at the Firestone plant. His arms were always black up to the elbow. I knew I didn't want to do that all my life. I swore I was going to school." To the University of Minnesota, it turned out, on a football scholarship, and there Dungy set most of the school's passing records. As pleasing to his parents, he graduated with a degree in business administration in 1977.

Like most schools, Minnesota did not use a pro-style passing game but employed Dungy as a sprint-out quarterback with the option to run, hand off, or pass while moving. In this kind of offense the quarterback is required to be an excellent athlete, and more frequently from the mid-1970s on, a black athlete. But when some of these black players were brought into the NFL, it was generally on the basis of athletic aptitude, not quarterbacking skills. They usually were drafted in a low round and became defensive backs, if they succeeded at all.

Dungy was torn. He wanted to see if he could play quarterback in the pros, but he had a chance to do that only if he went to play in Canada, where black quarterbacks like Warren Moon and Condredge Holloway were given a chance to play their college position, the league's overriding need for talent acting as a check on discrimination. Dungy wasn't drafted but went to camp with the Steelers in 1977 as a free agent. "I could have made three times as much in Canada and played quarterback, but I just had to see if I could make it in the NFL. It was the standard by which the best athletes were judged."

Tony made the Steelers' roster as a second-string safety. The '77 team was loaded with talent; Dungy was playing behind Mel Blount and Donnie Shell, which meant he wasn't playing much. "When I made the team, they offered me twenty thousand dollars. I certainly didn't have any bargaining position. What they offered, I took." And Tony Dungy was in the NFL.

Because Warren Moon, for example, went to Canada expressly to play quarterback, honed his skills there, and then came back to play the position well with the Houston Oilers, Dungy has had reason to rethink his choice. "Every now and then I'll wonder if I could have made it at quarterback here if I really got the chance to play. I didn't have the sheer arm strength they're always looking for, but I've seen some successful quarterbacks who weren't overpowering. They found ways to compensate. I say to myself when I see some of them now, 'I could have done that.' And more and more I wish I had gotten the chance."

It's not completely true that Dungy did not play quarterback in the NFL, and he will chat at length with anyone who wants to hear about his golden moments. "It was in my first season and Bradshaw had been hurt early in the game. We're at the Astrodome, losing to Houston seventeen to ten at the end of the third quarter, and Mike Kruczek, the backup, went down too. It was third down and Noll called me over and told me to run a quarterback keeper. We didn't make a first down and had to punt. If we had made the first down, I don't know what I would have called. When I got back in again, I started to throw the ball." There was no miracle comeback. If there had been, Dungy might not be a defensive coordinator today. The Steelers lost 24–10. "I was three for eight. One more catch and I would have been a fifty-percent NFL passer. One of my passes was dropped," he says, still slightly disappointed.

That first season with the Steelers offered a lesson in football and human nature Dungy wouldn't forget. Professional football has a psychological dimension as great as, if not greater than, the purely physical. "We had all that great talent," Dungy recalls, "but there were lots of problems. Players unhappy over money mostly. Teams we were better than just simply beat us. The very next year, about three weeks into training camp, I called my mom and told her to save her money, we were going to go to Miami and the Super Bowl for sure. We basically had all the same players, but the money problems had been taken care of. Everyone was happy. And we won the Super Bowl."

That season Dungy made $24,000. His Super Bowl share, however, was a stunning $32,000. "There was also a two-thousand-dollar bonus in my contract if I had played in fifty percent of the defensive downs. I only played in forty-one percent, but Mr. Rooney paid me anyway. It was a nice gesture and I appreciated it." Nothing seems to take the meanness out of a mean game like a little generosity and winning a Super Bowl.

But Dungy's glory was to be short-lived. The Steelers waived him in '79 and he caught on as a backup with the San Francisco 49ers, who traded him to the New York Giants the following year. He couldn't make the team, and no other NFL team was interested. Tony Dungy's brief but eventful NFL career was over—his playing career, that is.

Noll, who had spotted some coaching potential in Dungy, hired him in '81 as a defensive assistant. It would be the beginning of an apprenticeship. Dungy was twenty-five. He became the secondary coach the following season and defensive coordinator the year after, an unprecedented promotion for a twenty-seven-year-old. He was on track to accomplish some remarkable things.

It didn't take a genius to realize that Dungy's chief virtue, even as a player, was his mind. Talk to him even briefly and you're struck by his soft- and slow-spoken rationality, and particularly by the crystal-clear intelligence that seems to be reflected in his oversized brown eyes.

Rarely has Tony Dungy's name come up in the national media without some comment about the likelihood of his becoming the NFL's first black head coach. Tony has mixed feelings about such talk. Naturally, he's flattered he's considered qualified for the job; however, since he's heard it for almost five years now without him or any other black man breaking the barrier, the subject has become a source of frustration as much as flattery.

"If it happens, it happens," he says now with a shrug. "You just can't force things like that. I know one thing, though. If a head coaching job ever is offered to me, I'm not going to jump at it just because I'm black or just because I want to be a head coach. I don't want to find myself in a situation where I'm doomed to fail. What would that prove?

"No, it's got to be the right situation, the right sort of organization, with a compatible philosophy. I'd have to know how they drafted, what role the coach had, who had final say. It would have to be in a town where my family can be happy. No, I'd never do it just to take a shot at it."

Dungy has been interviewed twice for head coaching jobs. "One was a serious interview. One wasn't. That was at Green Bay. The serious interview was at Philadelphia in '85. I studied up on the history of the franchise and knew everything about the Eagles. I had a good discussion with Harry Gamble, the GM. Never got to talk to the team president. I knew the Eagles wanted Buddy Ryan for the job, but they were interviewing just in case things didn't work out." So even Dungy's "serious" interview was just a contingency.

The thing, above all others, that Dungy took from the two Steelers teams he played on was that even great talent can be short-circuited when the rage, the will, the focus weaken. Stoking the fire of desire and making sure there is a sense of unity are the tasks of a team's leaders. Sometimes that leadership comes from the head coach and his staff, but not very often these days. That run-through-the-wall-for-the-coach stuff ends in college, if not earlier.

Without an internal sense of direction, an NFL team, especially a young team in which new leadership has not yet had a chance to take root, is lost. Without strong leaders, a team will not develop a collective personality. It will be utterly without character, like the Tampa Bay Buccaneers or any of those teams from make-believe towns. It won't be a team at all, just a collection of players.

"Most of our young guys can play football," Dungy explains. "They've established that in college, in training camp. They're fine athletes. But so are the guys they're playing against. One of the things that helps you compete well is a sense of cohesion, the knowledge that you're part of something bigger and deeper than yourself, that if you have a lapse there's someone there to pick it up for you.

On the great Steelers teams, on any great team, there is such a deep sense of pride you can almost cut it with a knife, and it always comes from the team's leaders."

On most good professional teams, leaders emerge from among the players themselves. Most of the time, they are the team's best—the toughest, the gutsiest, the smartest, the coolest under pressure; in short, the heroes. Football is still a sport with real heroes, in the ancient Greek sense of the word—someone touched by the gods. The best players do not automatically become the leaders, not by a long shot; there are great players in the league who are as much resented by their teammates for their characters as admired for their talent. Conversely, on almost every team there is a leader who does not possess much natural talent but transcends it through effort and will.

How and which players emerge as team leaders is a mystery. They certainly do not nominate themselves, and they are not elected by constituencies. They simply possess admirable qualities as men and football players that make other football players want to emulate them, to be in their magnetic fields. Because the overworked analogy between football and war is so commonplace, you hear a team leader described as "a guy I'd follow into combat." Yes, there are large doses of respect and trust and admiration involved, but there is something more, something not so readily admitted. These players are *loved,* in a way that men can feel love for other men, even though they're not comfortable admitting it.

As with love and marriage, the relationship between a team and its leaders is a private matter, playing-field and locker-room stuff, for the most part. The leaders the media selects are not always the same ones the players recognize. And that, too, can be a source of internal strife. The media requires talkers; the players demand doers. The media gravitates to quarterbacks; players respect professionalism and heroism regardless of position.

Says Dungy, "On the old Steelers"—that phrase haunts Pittsburgh football lexicon like Englishmen talking about the Empire—"Terry Bradshaw was the spokesman." Dungy does not say "leader." Brad was outrageously talented and equally quotable. "But the defense had great leaders. Joe Greene. Jack Lambert. Jack Ham." Each for different reasons, it turns out. Ham was a quiet linebacker, one of the smartest men to play the position, but with great powers of anticipation and an almost unerring sense of doing the right thing.

Lambert was a beast, capable of ferocity on such a level that teammates stood open-mouthed when he turned it on. When Lambert maintained that level of intensity game after game, season after season, redefining for his teammates what desire was, awe became love and everyone's performance went up at least a notch.

Tunch Ilkin shakes his head in disbelief when reminiscing about Joe Greene's leadership. "Joe had a stare that was a physical presence. I remember a game my first year. We got beat. One of the guys alongside me was pulling off his uniform and fooling around a little too loud. Joe's locker was almost across the room and I saw him getting angry because the guy wasn't acting right. People don't believe me, but here's what I saw: Joe started staring at the guy's back, and after a few seconds the player stopped like he'd been tapped on the shoulder. He turned around and looked right across at Joe. Then he just dressed fast and got out." I've seen that look; I'd been struck by it in the coaches' film room. Everyone who knows Joe Greene knows that look.

Long before the season started, Dungy told me he thought the team could be solid and play around .500. But he had his doubts about making a playoff spot. When I asked why, he was more guarded in his optimism than most. "Just something I can't quite put my finger on," he said. "I guess it has to do with the personalities of most of our players. First, we have very few really mean guys. Now, I know that not all mean guys are tough. But I'm also concerned that we don't have a whole lot of tough guys. And *all* tough guys are tough. It's from the really tough guys that your core of leaders usually comes."

During training camp and the preseason, the whole coaching staff became increasingly aware that any potential leaders were slow to emerge. They saw it as a serious problem, but they also knew that patience and a heroic victory or two would do more to let leaders sort themselves out than anything they could do to try to push matters along.

"Since leaders don't seem to have developed," I asked Dungy one afternoon before an early-season practice, "why don't the coaches sort of promote leadership in subtle ways? Chuck's been around long enough to spot players who have the potential."

"It doesn't work that way on a football team. There's a complicated system of choices that's involved. If you start tampering, you could have yourself some very serious personality problems, a heck of a lot worse that what we've got now. All a coach can do is put certain guys in leadership positions and encourage them. They'll respond or they won't. Chuck's been doing that, but some of the key guys are hurt or haven't proven themselves to their teammates yet."

Five games into the season, when the leadership still had not emerged, I would ask Dungy, "What if leaders don't ever develop?"

"Then we've got ourselves a team without a heck of a lot of character."

Had the Steelers only hung on to that lead in Washington and had Bubby hit Rodney Carter when he was open against Cincinnati, this collection could be on its way to becoming a team. But "had onlys" are "ifs," and "ifs" are wishes, and wishes don't get answered very often in the NFL, especially on have-not teams; so, far into the season the new Steelers would still be a collection looking for leaders.

Some of the Steelers' best veterans happened to be quiet, almost shy men. Linebackers Bryan Hinkle and David Little were admirable players but close to being introverts; Hinkle had been particularly withdrawn in 1988 because he played hurt much of the previous two seasons. Mike Merriweather would undoubtedly have been one of the team leaders, but he was no longer on this team. Keith Willis had nearly developed the stature and confidence as a player to have filled part of the vacuum; he was tough and mean. So the Steelers lost more than a pass rusher when he went down on the third day of training camp.

Certainly the team's two Super Bowl veterans, Mike Webster and Dwayne Woodruff, could have chosen to step forward. They did not. Both were nearing the end of their careers, and had other things on their minds.

There was some anger in the Steelers' front office that Webster opted to remain a distant elder statesman rather than a take-charge guy. And Noll got upset with Woodruff for looking ahead to a postfootball career as a lawyer at the expense of his team's leadership needs. Both players were also preoccupied with trying to remain proficient enough to keep their starting jobs.

Tunch Ilkin seemed the perfect candidate—experienced, outgoing, wise, a fine player—but he was the team's union representative. In a sense, that's already a formal leadership position; Tunch was the shop steward, which was how most of the players saw him. The position did give him a certain authority, but it also subtly robbed him of the freedom to act too independently, a quality natural team leaders must have.

Bubby Brister appeared to have the carriage and the inclination, and his audacity was impressive. But it was far too early to tell about his stature. Besides, he hadn't proved absolutely he could cut it at quarterback and hadn't really paid his dues yet, and until he did, he risked being a braggart who could disqualify himself from leadership in the future. His boundless enthusiasm, however, was infectious; it wasn't leadership, but at least it was something. For much of the season, it would be all the Steelers had.

Delton Hall, because of his style of play his rookie year, could have been a candidate, but his injured, tentative play had taken away much of his confidence; he was having trouble leading himself. Rod Woodson was an unquestionable talent, a meteor on the field, excitable, passionate, and unpredictable. But he lacked a personal solidity and selflessness. Those qualities might come in time, but right now he was too immature.

The player I had felt intuitively could grow to leadership a few years down the line was Dermontti Dawson (maybe it was the name that got me), a rookie, second-round draft choice from the University of Kentucky. He was listed as an offensive guard but would play very little in the first half of the season because of strained knee ligaments. He was, admittedly, a long shot, for I had no tangible indication that Dawson could even play in the league. But he had a royal presence. Not a talker, but an intense listener and observer, Dawson had a strong, silent strength about him, a quality that cannot be faked and is rare in so young a man. Joe Greene had it as a rookie. When Dawson would finally overcome his injuries and get into the lineup, he would identify himself as a "player." Noll saw him as one of the season's bright lights. He was tabbed as a future leader.

A lack of leadership is not the only team personality problem Dungy sees developing this season. He admits, "Yes, we're asking our guys to do a lot. And, yes, there have been mistakes out there, and we've been burned. But they seem to have assimilated things well enough. We've simply got to begin to cut down on our mistakes. If we do, we'll eventually be all right."

Wondering if things haven't gotten too sophisticated for a sport so elemental, I ask, "When you get right down to it, isn't talent the thing—can't it overcome just about anything?"

Dungy responds in a flash. "Not really. All it does on this level is give you more margin for error. But this team is not deep. There isn't the amount of talent here that the top-echelon teams have. So we have to play with even fewer errors to be competitive game after game. What I look for above all is a smart and a tempered player."

For Dungy and the coaching staff the success of this season will really be measured by how many "smart and tempered" NFL players develop. It is a little too early to tell who they are and how many of them there will be eventually.

Complicated as such an evaluation would seem to be, in the NFL it is reduced to a weekly numerical grade. "It's really a pretty basic thing," Dungy explains. "You run film, look at each player in your unit on every play, and decide if he made the right choices and then executes them properly. If he does, you give him a plus on that play; if not, a minus. The number of pluses divided into the total number of plays gives you his percentage, and that's his grade. Chuck believes eighty percent from every player is winning football." Grading players is also part of the coaches' Monday responsibilities.

The system works better for some positions than for others. "The assignments of offensive linemen are so specific, the statistic makes some sense. They make the block or they don't. It's measurable and it really matters to them."

The Monday after Game Four, a no-sacks-allowed game against Buffalo, guard Terry Long, a moody, impertinent man, is ecstatic. He's gotten his grade from Hal Hunter, his coach, and it's a good one. "See here," he boasts, pointing to the running account of the game. "Slow off the ball twice. Blew the running play right here. But I was in there for sixty-three plays. Just three mistakes for yours truly. An eighty-five! I'll take that every Monday till I retire."

From across the locker room a voice: "Keep bragging like that and we'll retire you in practice this week."

"The system doesn't really apply to my people, though," says Dungy, "because a guy can make two mistakes, but those mistakes could cost a ball game. That's why I try to factor in defensive breakdowns also to give a more honest picture of what happened. Then there's the problem of how to tell a player his grade. Basically, it's a teaching decision. Sometimes I'll call a guy in, sometimes I'll tell the entire group. It depends on the maturity of the individual and what the effect is going to be on the team. Generally with this group, I low-key the grade. They got to be brought along delicately."

From training camp, Dungy knew he had, with the exception of Dwayne Woodruff, a very young secondary and an inexperienced defense overall. What concerned him were the signs that they were immature as well. "The difference between young and immature is whether they can learn from their mistakes and how fast." So far the signs have been bad. Some players make the same mistakes repeatedly. Sometimes, when the defensive backs are supposed to rotate counterclockwise, Woodson misses the assignment or responds too late to be effective. Even when Woodson gets it, sometimes Delton Hall forgets.

Generally, Dungy expects his players to know all their assignments but, beyond that, to understand what the defense as a whole is attempting to do strategically so they will be able to adjust in unexpected situations. He is trying to teach his young players that for seasoned secondaries, as for wise, mature adults, there are no unexpected situations.

Frankly, on the eve of Game Four, he believes progress is too slow.

8

NOLL PUTS HIS NAME ON IT

Waiting at the Pittsburgh airport with all its assertive "most livable" banners, tense men are milling around trying to feel a little less tense. Dennis Fitzgerald, the special teams coach, is demonstrating a brush-block technique on Greg Lloyd. On a Noll team with so many young players, teaching is an ongoing activity.

Even when the Bills were a poor team, no one wanted to go up to Buffalo to play them. The weather. From November on it is bitter cold, usually with snow. Even if you have to play them early in the year, there are terrible winds to contend with. The weather this time is perfect; it is the mental state of the Steelers that is turbulent. They have lost two games they could and perhaps should have won. Injuries have piled on previous injuries; there are more holes than ever, more inexperienced players thrown into the breech. No one knows how they'll respond.

How deep are their own doubts? Will they play not to lose rather than to win? The difference is that fraction of a second between immediate football instinct and the thoughtful moment when you don't want to make a mistake, that moment precisely when the mistake is conceived. Winners play naturally, losers self-consciously. The Bills are on their game. Maybe the Steelers will get lucky. That would equalize everything.

On the field, all the answers come quickly. Brister fumbles the second snap of the game, turning it over to the Bills with field position. Jim Kelly throws an apparent touchdown pass, but instant replay, "the eye in the sky" that Noll detests, overrules, and the Bills settle for a field goal.

On the next Bills series, Dwayne Woodruff intercepts Kelly, apparently a big play turnaround. But the Steelers have twelve defensive men on the field at the time, the unmistakable sign of poor management and irresponsibility. There is no more glaring symptom of ineptitude as not knowing who the hell is supposed to be on the field. Whose fault? Blame will be assigned later. After a penalty is stepped off, the Bills score.

It gets worse. After Pittsburgh recovers a fumble at their own 31 and can't advance, Harry Newsome's punt is blocked cleanly, setting up another Bills field goal. Punts should not be blocked, certainly not by a player coming in untouched. Who gets blamed for that one?

Not only bad play but bad luck mocks the Steelers. Reserve cornerback Larry Griffin intercepts Kelly on the Steelers' 10 and has a clear path down the sideline for a 90-yard touchdown. At the 25 his stride shortens, at the 35 he limps, and he hops out of bounds and falls to the ground at the 43. Untouched, Griffin had developed a charley horse and had to quit on a sure touchdown run. The Flies up in the press box howl to the heavens and ask one another if they've ever seen a play like that before. They haven't. "Snakebit" is an expression the Steelers are going to invoke frequently in the weeks ahead.

It gets worst. There's still a chance to pull close in the second half, but a second Newsome punt is blocked. A Jackson fumble kills another drive. Too late, Brister makes the final score (36–28 Buffalo) respectable with some excellent long passes directly into a prevent defense.

Afterward, Brister says the obvious: "We lost it because of ourselves. We're beating ourselves out of games every week. If I knew why we make all these mistakes, I'd do something about it. But I don't. Frankly, it mystifies the shit out of me."

With a quarter of the season gone, Bubby has absorbed a pretty good physical beating. "It sure would be easier to take if we were winning. I'm full of aches and pains all the time. Damn artificial turf. It's a killer. God bless this flak jacket." He slips out of his padded vest, which he credits for keeping rushers from collapsing the basic skeletal structure of his body. "I won't be all the way well till around February."

In the drafty visiting team's locker room at Rich Stadium, the players tend to take deep breaths and grimace before responding even to reasonable questions. They answer as succinctly as possible. There is too much control, too much resistance, even for a team that has lost its third straight. An outburst of rage would be refreshingly honest.

Second-year special teams player Tyronne Stowe was most responsible for the first of Newsome's blocked punts. When I tell him the guy who made the block bragged about how bad he'd beaten Stowe, I expect at least hostility. Stowe says, "He was lucky and he knows it."

Noll always reminds his players it's a long season; he wants them to try to keep an even keel, not get too high in victory, too low in defeat, especially early in the season. But there doesn't seem to be a well of emotion here that has to be controlled. It is normally the task of a team's leaders to make sure emotion builds, but this team doesn't have leaders.

Tony Dungy is temperate, as always, but worried: "Not much you can do but keep on keeping on, but if we don't get some breaks soon, it could get bad."

This crop of Steelers is, with few exceptions, a reserved bunch. Far from demonstrative when winning in preseason and when staying competitive in their early games, they've become somber, almost morose in defeat. Of course, most of them are hurting physically, but where is their indignation and anger? The Steelers appear to be going quietly.

The sun is sinking magnificently over Lake Erie as the bus rolls toward the airport. Players are silent. Some are scanning the stat sheet, hoping to hide behind their numbers when performances are evaluated tomorrow, their day off. Those who haven't made gross, naked errors hurt for the guys who have, but they're also grateful they won't be pointed out.

I'm sitting next to Jim Kriek, a crusty older writer for the Uniontown paper. Kriek has a crew cut and a raw face that doesn't seem to coincide at all with his penchant for quoting Shakespeare.

"What would Shakespeare have said about this one?" I ask.

"The Bard wouldn't want to get involved with a mess like this."

Tunch Ilkin is usually an emotional man, but he too has caught the melancholies. He knows he's been playing well, and that makes losing even harder to swallow. He and his wife are expecting their second child; he confesses after a midweek practice, "I usually look forward to going to the Lamaze classes with Sharon, but it's not going to be easy showing my face if things don't change. At least the baby's coming along fine; the dilation is perfectly normal."

GAME DAY 5: SUNDAY, OCTOBER 2

Cleveland (2-2) at Pittsburgh (1-3)

The general hope is that Buffalo was as bad as it gets. In their hearts, smart people can recognize such downward spirals, into which we've all been pulled at various times in our lives. Those damn things seem to have a momentum all their own and end only when they're completely played out and not a moment before. Not much you can do about it but keep trying your best and looking for something to believe in, a sign perhaps that the bad luck is over.

The young men hawking $20 tickets around the ballpark are happy to get $12.

I don't even have to ask Frank Krupka what he thinks; he volunteers. "I feel kind of stupid saying this is a very big game for this team. I know I said that last time. Both times it's been true, though. I honestly believe if they had beat Washington, they would have beat Cincinnati too. Even after losing to Washington, the Cincinnati game could have got them believing in themselves again. Now they got to stop the slide. This is such an emotional game, football. If they don't there's no telling how low they might sink. No telling." He looks straight down below Pittsburgh toward the center of the earth.

I ask Krupka how he accounts for all the incredibly dumb, embarrassing mistakes.

"Did you ever go through one of those times when you screw up everything? Lock yourself out of the house. Lose your car keys. Forget important appointments. I made a goddamned apple pie last Sunday and forgot to take it out of the oven while I was watching the game. When I remembered, I thought I saved it just in time. You know what I discovered? I forgot to rinse out the pie tin and the whole damn thing tasted like soap. Had to throw it out."

"Think we ought to throw this team out too?" I ask him.

"Can't. They're all we got. When you have these pitfalls, you want to avoid them at all costs and almost just because of that, you fall right in. Only thing can turn it around for them is a good old-fashioned, convincing Pittsburgh Stillers win over their arch-rival, the hated Cleveland Browns, heh, heh."

There is a hopeful sign today. Bernie Kosar, the Browns' masterly quarterback, is out with an elbow injury. His backup is out as well, so the Browns go with Mike Pagel, their third-string. That levels the playing field quite a bit, maybe even tips it in favor of the Steelers.

Brister, who has begun the long process of establishing himself in the league and as the Pittsburgh quarterback of the nineties, had career highs in every passing category against Buffalo. He also played very well two weeks earlier, in Washington. What the coaching staff wants from Brister now is consistency, a level of performance below which he does not slip.

Against the Browns he's dreadful. So are most of the Steelers and many of the Browns. Only because Gary Anderson, the Steelers' placekicker, is among the best, does Pittsburgh lead 9–7 at halftime.

Late in the third quarter, Brister rolls out of the pocket and is hit from behind just as he releases the ball. He falls face forward under the tackler, with his throwing hand pinned under him. His middle finger is bent out of shape. On a team that is nothing but plugged holes, the biggest hole of all suddenly appears. The announcement in the press box is: "Bubby Brister has injured his throwing hand and will not return."

Before he is injured, Brister has thrown three "pigs." He is re-placed by Steve Bono, who throws one of his own in the last quarter that is run back for a touchdown that ices the game for the Browns. At the bitter end, while the Browns line up for an irrelevant final field goal, one of the Pittsburgh ground crew is cursing as he pulls up the net that will keep the football from being lost in the stands: "These fucking play calls! Chuck's so goddamned conservative. Always tell just what he's gonna do. They're gonna want his head tomorrow morning. Shit, they should have had it years ago."

Boos reverberate as the Steelers come off the field. It is a sound that has not often been directed at the players in black and gold in the history of this stadium. The fans who stay are angry, and with good reason. The Steelers have not only played badly and without inspiration; the game plan was uninteresting and ineffective in its very conception.

Chuck Noll hardly ever gives anything away in his postgame press conference, but he slips this time. Someone asks him about the similarities between this and the 1-13 season of '69. He says, "Some good things came of that season—the players we drafted." Noll is thinking about the draft. Playoff thoughts are dead.

The worst news is that two of Brister's fingers are dislocated. Even while he was in there, it was clear that he had to play extremely well all season for the Steelers to be competitive. Without him, there's no telling how bad things could get.

As I walk to my car, I hear throughout the parking lot, "This season's gone." It it a refrain picked up immediately on the radio as I flip to Cope's show on 1250 AM. Caller after caller says he's had it with the Stillers, with a second-rate organization fielding second-rate players, with Chuck Noll's old-fashioned way of playing football.

Myron reminds them about the 1976 season, when the Steelers lost four of their first five. But that team surprised everyone, including Myron. In the last week of the season, they still had an outside chance of making the playoffs. Myron felt so sure they'd miss, he went on the air and said he'd swim the Mon in midwinter if the team got in. They did, and, in fact, got to the AFC championship game.

Myron, insulated by a wet suit and with a boat full of lifeguards hovering nearby, went in the water under the cameras and lights of his evening telecast. "When you do something as stupid as that, you want proof; otherwise they'll make you do it again." Myron set a longevity record getting to the other side.

None of his callers on this day believe the 1988 Steelers can make the same turnaround. Neither does Myron.

Pittsburgh resigns itself to another empty season.

GAME DAY 6: SUNDAY, OCTOBER 9

Pittsburgh (1-4) at Phoenix (3-2)

It is an equatorial 117 degrees on the playing field at game time. The slide is on. Not even a Steelers loyalist expects a victory. Even with an erratic Brister at the tiller, the offense had been badly adrift and out of its depth. Todd Blackledge will start at quarterback. Steve Bono will play if he falters. Things do not figure to improve during Brister's enforced absence. A respectable showing will be a positive enough sign for now.

Early in the game Rod Woodson returns a kickoff 92 yards to tie the score at seven. The Steelers will not score another point until late in the last quarter. In between, everything is Phoenix execution and Steelers ineptitude. A statistical example: Pittsburgh penalties— 10 (3 give first downs); Phoenix—1. Total yards: Phoenix—388; Steelers—203.

"They could have beat us fifty to nothing," free safety Thomas Everett says afterward. Phoenix settles for 31–14.

In the third quarter, team president Dan Rooney had walked out of the press box to stare into the desert and hope for a vision. With Rooney out of earshot, one of the Flies said, "You can run, Dan, but you can't hide." When he came back inside, Rooney estimated, "We're pretty close to bottom now."

Sam Nover, the WPXI-TV sportscaster, asked the press box at large, "When's the last time you've seen a Steelers team *this* bad?"

Silence. Reflection. Then Jim Kriek's foghorn: "Last week!" Joyless, uproarious laughter.

There is no laughter in the dressing room. In fact, there are tears. Delton Hall can barely speak, he is so full of emotion. There is an involuntary quiver in his cheek as he tries to keep his composure. The physical pain is great; he played with the groin pull and twice reinjured the wrist. And although he played in a new position, strong safety, the result was the same: Again he was beaten for a touchdown pass and another pass that set up a score. "It hurts so much," he says finally; he is speaking about much more than the wrist, the groin, and the touchdown.

The running game has just about disappeared. Against the Cardinals, the Steelers ran for a total of 78 yards. In the *Press*, Steve Hubbard will feature the deficiency under the head STEELERS BACKS CAN'T RUN AWAY FROM FAILURE.

Noll lets it be known that the Steelers' long practice sessions— among the longest in the league—are going to get even longer next week.

There is, I hate to admit, a morbid fascination in watching exactly how bad this team's tailspin can get.

GAME DAY 7: SUNDAY, OCTOBER 16
Houston (4-2) at Pittsburgh (1-5)

For Noll, today is rock bottom. It isn't only losing 34–14. It's losing to the Houston Oilers. It's losing with the added humiliation of not being able to get the right number of players on the field on two different occasions, and getting called for seven offsides. It is a total team collapse, of the mind as well as of the spirit and the flesh.

In 1987, after the Oilers whacked the Steelers good, Noll met Oilers coach Jerry Glanville at midfield and, in the presence of cameras and microphones, accused Glanville of teaching and encouraging dirty football. Noll was saying directly to the source what some other coaches around the league had been whispering. It looked like a sore loser's pettiness, especially since Noll's great teams had been vicious intimidators as well—but clean ones, Noll would argue.

Glanville says he used that incident to psyche his team up for today's game. "We knew who we were facing. I sent them out with a two-word message. But we'll keep those two words to ourselves." My guess is the second word was "Noll."

The Oilers are really an obnoxious football team—chippy, taunting cheap-shot artists. They are turning on all their worst qualities today as though to rub Noll's nose in it. After cornerback Cris Dishman blocks yet another of Newsome's punts, he pats Newsome on the fanny and blows him a big kiss. Typical of an Oilers game, fights break out all afternoon, and there are late hits, pilings on—things that would have hurt the Oilers if they weren't so comfortably ahead.

In the press box Ketchman is livid after a late Houston hit out of bounds. He's disgusted at the Steelers. "These guys have quit. I saw Jack Lambert on the sidelines once take a thirty-yard run at a guy who did that to one of his teammates." It's a sign of the times in Pittsburgh that they still have to invoke Jack Lambert's name.

The headline on Gene Collier's column in the *Press* will read: THIS MESS CARRIES NOLL'S NAME ON IT. And Noll will, in fact, take the blame—"When you lose a game like this, there's nobody who can take refuge anyplace. There's no question attitude is my job, crispness is my job, and we certainly weren't that." It is a stand-up thing to take personal responsibility for a team gone bad. It also gets stale very fast when you have to do it week after week.

Glanville says, before he leaves Pittsburgh, "I had no intention of shaking hands with him. He got me once; he won't get me twice."

There is no apparent way to hold this team together. Some vehement callers on Cope's show are asking for Noll's head, and there are more of them than ever before. They sound like older men, not come-lately Steelers fans impatient with the mediocrity of the eighties. These are people who know what Noll has meant to this franchise.

In previous years, when Mark Malone was driving fans over the edge with poor play, the TV and radio stations regularly ran quarterback popularity polls; the fans called or wrote in with their choice for quarterback. Malone never won, but Noll stuck with him—out of spite, some Flies will tell you. Most of the stations are talking now about running a "Dump Noll" poll. None of them ever go that far, partly out of respect for Noll's record but more out of fear that such Noll-bashing might backfire. It's too early. The bashers might get bashed. There is still too much quiet loyalty for Charles Henry Noll in this city.

Still, with the team at 1-6, I would have taken an odds-on bet that this was Chuck Noll's last season as coach of the Steelers.

"You know how people are always saying you got to have belief," reserve defensive back Lupe Sanchez says. "I've always had belief, in myself, in this team. But after you play your heart out and you got nothing to show for it, about the only belief you have left is *dis*belief."

WHEN PROUD MEN FAIL

After the Houston loss, Tunch Ilkin tells each and every reporter who stops by his cubicle, "One thing I know for sure—there's no quit or backing up in any man in this room." Of course he can't know that; only each person knows it in his secret self.

Privately, Tunch admits, "I know I've said it a hundred times and it sounds like B.S., but I refuse to just let everything fall apart. I've got to be positive. But, believe me, we're really hurting. It's almost like everyone is waiting for bad things to happen out there, and sure enough they do. There's no confidence left at all. I don't know what rock bottom might be, but this'll do until it comes along."

All losses aren't the same. Each one has a different quality. Some, like Washington, stick like a sharp pain in the ribs and leave the taste of gall on the tongue. Cleveland was a clubbing and felt like an accumulation of body blows, none of which stands out, that left a deep overall soreness and the taste of spoiled meat. And not only does each loss have a feel and taste of its own, there is a cumulative effect as well. Rock bottom, the sixth consecutive loss, to the Houston Oilers no less, feels leaden, a dulling heaviness that makes movement impossible. It tastes metallic.

"I feel," Tunch admits, "I have a responsibility not to slink away. I've got to answer all their questions as honestly as I can while still being loyal to my teammates. But I swear to God, I don't know what to say because I don't know what's gone wrong."

When Ilkin invokes God's name, it requires a bit of an explanation. Like Dungy, he's a prominent member of one of the Steelers' Bible-study groups. But Tunch is a convert to Christianity. Born in Istanbul, Turkey, he grew up a Muslim. His mother was Miss Turkey of 1950. His small, authoritarian father ruled with an iron hand.

Tunch, it seemed, was always adjusting. The family moved to Chicago when he was two years old. He learned to cope with the hard ways of hard streets without becoming hard himself. When the family moved to the suburbs, Tunch thought the good life was the toughest adjustment of all. "No 'enemy' neighborhoods, none of the dangers of street gangs or trouble in the schoolyard. I was so used to all that stuff, I thought living in the suburbs was really too weird."

At Indiana State he was drawn to beliefs other than his father's. "I guess I was always asking myself the purpose of things in this world. Finally, Christianity offered me the answers. But there was no way I could ever tell my father. He's only about five feet seven, but he's, you know, *the father*. I was afraid to confront him about it. Eventually he found out about it, and he was the one who came to me and said, 'Why couldn't you tell me?'

"What we are going through this season is so incredible, so hard, I swear I don't know how the guys who *aren't* religious can handle it. Even at its best, this world, if you really look at it, is maddening."

Tunch has been sorely tested this season. He is known among his peers throughout the league to have willed and pushed himself into becoming one of the better offensive tackles in the game. Yet he has played on losing teams two of his last three seasons and feels deprived of the success and recognition such effort ought to bring. And he's performed with nagging pain all season, taking cortisone shots in both his shoulders to get him through games and even some of the rougher practices. He minimizes that: "You know what L. C. Greenwood used to say? 'Hell, anyone can play this game healthy.' "

Ilkin's first years overlapped Greenwood's final ones. He knows that somewhere down the line his body will pay for this abuse. "Let's just say that it's a price I'm willing to pay to do what I'm doing. I know it's not a rational thing, but when you're part of a team effort of so many guys making sacrifices to try to do something really difficult—the feeling, well, it can't really be explained. In my heart I believe we're building something here. It'll take awhile, but I like being a part of it. It puts me in the footsteps of some great men who were doing it when I got here. Sure, sometimes I feel the way we're playing it isn't worth it, but those negative feelings always pass, or at least they have so far."

When he arrives home, his wife, Sharon, who is nursing their brand-new daughter, Natalie, will eventually want to hear about the Houston game. Tunch drives home in his pickup truck, arriving after six. He opens a can of cold beer almost immediately. Sharon hasn't watched the game but has heard the result. Tanner, his three-year-old, will want to wrestle before bed like always, and Tunch will oblige, sore shoulders, sore hands, and all. It's not until the kids go to sleep that Tunch can really begin to unwind.

Later, over a steak and vegetables, Sharon will ask about the team: "Things were so promising in camp, in the preseason—what's gone wrong?"

That's the same question all the Flies want the answer to. And still Tunch doesn't know exactly. He knows that when they couldn't win some of those close games early, almost like a leaky tire, something just went out of them—perhaps the possibility of believing in themselves.

"Today was different," he says. "We seemed flat going into the game. Even though it was the Oilers and they were doing their usual number, we stayed flat. We all stunk collectively. Why? I swear I don't know."

After Sharon goes to sleep, Tunch turns on the TV. He watches until 3 A.M. "I don't remember a single thing I saw. I say I watched, but I just sat there and stared until my body told me it was time to get into the bed. Losing like this does strange things to your mind."

The next day Tunch has some complicated business to take care of at the bank. He's so ashamed of how the team played, he postpones much of it and settles for a deposit at the automated teller. Even there, he pulls the bill of his red cap over his face.

Dwayne Woodruff, the cornerback who played in Super Bowl XIV, also feels humiliated after this recent loss. Woodruff has been going to the Duquesne University law school nights and during the off-season for four years. Noll and the front office have encouraged Woodruff's ambitions; it is positive publicity for the Steelers and professional football. Here was a good player showing what could be done through a combination of individual ambition and the encouragement of an enlightened organization. Noll has said more players ought to be as intelligent about their futures as Woodruff. In training camp, Woodruff studied not only his playbook but a thick Pennsylvania bar exam study guide as well.

Noll magnanimously gave Woodruff a couple of days off from training camp to go to Pittsburgh to take the test. Still awaiting the results with his team at 1-6, Woodruff says with unlawyerlike candor, "I can honestly say this season has been, without a doubt, the worst experience I've ever had in sports. It's humiliating going out there every week, getting stomped on and not showing very much improvement as a unit." The way things have been going, even chasing ambulances must look more attractive than chasing receivers.

Mike Webster, who has four Roman numerals on his résumé, evaluates the situation with his familiar elder statesman's perspective: "When football's going good—and that's the way it's been here most of the time for me—there's no other feeling like it in the world. My Lord, it's sweet. Conversely, the burden is unbearably heavy when times are like this. But if you're a man of pride, you keep trying. The real sin is not in having failed but in not having tried your level best, and I can't say I've seen any people who haven't been trying out there."

That's exactly what the Gipper's speechwriter would have had him say in the same situation, and there is some truth in it. But it doesn't satisfy the Flies, who want to know the how and the why of it all. How it began to come unraveled. And why.

After the loss to the Oilers, Gerald Williams, the second-year nose tackle whose cubicle is tucked behind the entranceway, looks philosophical while he adjusts his glasses. They make him look like a bebop musician. He's a gentle man in civilian clothes who always speaks in quiet tones. His expression is pained as he tries to explain with simple elegance how it feels and what he must do. "I've never gone through anything like this in my life. I've come to see it as a time of trial, personally and for all of us, but mostly personally. I've decided what I have to do about it. When I go home tonight, I'm going to have to get by myself and do some serious soul-searching."

Williams takes a deep breath. His voice has been getting softer as he speaks. "Every football player knows within himself what he can really do—I know I do. We've been listening to things outside ourselves; when that happens, you begin to lose your confidence. Without confidence, a football player shouldn't even be out there. It is the worst, most helpless feeling in the world. But if I begin to look into myself again, I can start to control what I *can* do, control how I *can* play. Then, if the other guys do the same thing—or even if they don't—maybe we can stop it. At least, maybe I can stop it for me. I don't want to go on living this way."

Moving around the room, I hear the players' true bewilderment come out as a series of predictable clichés. Thomas Everett, the free safety: "We're all playing hurt and there's just so much you can do when you can't go all out." Gregg Carr, linebacker: "Individually we seem to be trying to do too much and getting ourselves in even hotter water." Aaron Jones: "Snakebit. Just a little bit of bad luck at the beginning, then a little worse luck. Now, nothing can go right, we're snakebit." Terry Long: "'Course you got to keep trying, but when you're in a down cycle there's just not a hell of a lot can be done, 'cept wait it out."

Only Earnest Jackson, whose fumbles have bounced him out of a starting job, refuses to speak to the media. There are some Flies who believe that Jackson's blaming Brister for his handoff in Washington was a major breach of professional honor. Maybe the gods of professional football were so offended by it they have wreaked this havoc on the Steelers as punishment. They are stern gods.

Earnest doesn't have many friends on the team. Players sense he's trouble, a football Hessian. Jackson ran for over 1,000 yards at San Diego in '84 and was surprisingly traded to Philadelphia, where he duplicated the feat in '85 but was nevertheless waived by the Eagles in training camp the following year. Signed by the Steelers after the '86 season began, he ran at the same impressive over-1,000-yard pace, ending up with 910 yards in thirteen games. It is more than unusual for such an effective runner to be lateraled so often.

Proven thousand-yard NFL runners in their primes aren't exactly chopped liver. Yet here was one who because of a pair of loose lips and a vague fog of bad raps, was running out of teams who might want to buy his services. A Fly told me, "I've heard he's always been a problem in the locker room. Gets other players riled up; just a troublemaker and general pain in the ass. He was fine here his first season. Kept his mouth shut. But he's such a jerk. He scored a twenty-nine-yard TD against Dallas, and you know what he said? Should have given him the ball outside the thirty because he gets a bonus for every run of thirty yards or more. Strange, self-destructive man, this Earnest Jackson. He's probably doing the right thing not speaking to the press."

"We knew Earnest's track record when we signed him—on the field and in the locker room," a Steelers front-office official explains. "There was a pattern. But we needed an effective running back and we knew he could be that. We projected him for no more than three years, and this is his third. If he's here next year, it'll be a surprise. If he's here two more years, it'll be a miracle."

If Jackson is personally humiliated by the utter collapse of his football team, he doesn't show it, probably because it really isn't *his* team. It is *a* team. He began to separate himself physically from his teammates on the sideline when Noll pulled him out after one of his fumbles in the Phoenix game. Noll would keep him out more and more, eventually replacing him against Houston with Merril Hoge, a raw-boned country boy from Pocatello, Idaho, who came so low (tenth round) in the '87 draft, his making the team went beyond being a long shot. In his rookie year, Hoge carried the ball three times for eight yards—count 'em, eight.

There is a refreshing openness about Hoge. Maybe it's that he's more earnest than Earnest, more than most of the other guys in black and gold these days. Even though the team is playing poorly, Hoge has done some good running. At six feet two and 230, Hoge often breaks individual tackles and can make the pile fall backward when he's gang tackled, a promising sign. He's a strong blocker and a good pass catcher too. Jackson, at five-nine and 225, is your bowling-ball runner and not as adept a blocker or catcher as Hoge. Hoge is also six years younger than Jackson and can be bought a lot more cheaply: Jackson makes $475,000, Hoge $80,000.

One of the virtues of being up against it—if indeed this is really as bad as it gets—probably its only virtue, is that players and coaches must take serious stock of themselves. They are forced to reevaluate not only their talents but their character as well. Only fools would lie to themselves under these circumstances. It also gives the coaching staff a chance to evaluate players who ordinarily would not be getting the opportunity to play much in a more competitive season. Because the Steelers are going nowhere, even more rookies and second-year men than were projected in training camp—players normally relegated to special teams for a couple of seasons—are getting a chance to show what they can do, ready or not.

Merril Hoge is quietly content about the team's misfortunes. "I don't like that it came about the way it did, but I knew that if I just kept trying and did what the coaches asked of me, I'd get my chance eventually. It just came a little sooner this way. Once I got in and realized my future was in my own hands, I sure as heck wasn't going to let it slip away. I want to be here too much for that. Besides, this isn't the toughest job I've ever had in my life. You ever lay irrigation pipes on farmland? Then you don't know what real effort is. I like it here. It's fun." But remember, Merril, fun is winning!

Hoge, running backs Warren Williams, Dwight Stone, and Rodney Carter, linebackers Hardy Nickerson and Darin Jordan, offensive lineman Dermontti Dawson—none beyond his second year of professional football—are the young players whose stock has risen considerably because of the injuries and poor play of others. Performing under NFL pressure, they seem to pass muster much of the time. In some instances, they play excellently, but consistency is what they must master next. It's an ill wind indeed that doesn't blow somebody a bit of good. But mostly it blows the Steelers despair.

Merril Hoge spots me in the locker room after the loss to Houston, comes over, and says, "When I said playing here is fun, I want to be sure you know I didn't mean I didn't mind losing. Heck, I hate what's happening to us. It's just that at least I've got this chance to play."

I assure him that I understand, but 1-6 is making everyone look back over his shoulder.

*

There are few places on earth where being a loser marks you as deeply or leaves such a noticeable scar as in the good old U.S. of A. Losing, like being poor, is perceived here as an unforgivable weakness of character and a source not merely of disappointment but of shame. All this is intensified when the losing is football losing, when it is continual, and when it takes place in Pittsburgh.

Conversely, nowhere is winning so overvalued, as though it is always deserved, with luck never really entering fully into the equation. Since in Pittsburgh the Stillers' great tradition of success had gone beyond football and become a justification for the lives of so many people—the tens of thousands of men like Krupka the younger—not winning carries a special sinfulness. The specific sin is rarely uttered, but simply understood: It is betrayal.

When fine athletes are not only beaten but beaten badly, they suffer just like the rest of us, the only difference being the height from which they fall and the visibility that height imposes on them. Because they are proud men, they may put on a brave face for the world, but in the privacy of their homes, their private torment is no less tangible or painful.

"The team expects us to do public-service and charity appearances," says Bubby Brister. "It takes a lot of my time, but it's part of my responsibilities as one of the team's spokesmen, so I try to do what I can. Believe me, it's easier to do when you're winning. I get asked some very embarrassing questions about our record. Sometimes it's like going into hostile territory. When I get back to my apartment, I feel like I've been worked over by the Oilers."

Excellent athletes often appear larger than life, and we tend to think of them as apart from if not superior to it. And in terms of fame, income, and influence they may be. But in most essential ways, because youth and health and talent are so impermanent, life's cares are for them intensified along with life's rewards. Most of them know that their triumphs will soon become mere memories.

Fans can never fathom, for example, why star athletes would jeopardize exciting careers and large salaries with alcohol or drugs. You hear, "Hell, the guy's making half a million bucks, and he blows it messing with that stuff. He must be stupid." And that's precisely the point: He *is* stupid. People don't stop being stupid or vain or shallow or arrogant or cheap or dishonest or insensitive—or any other human flaw you can think of—just because they can catch a football in perfect stride, block a jump shot, or hum a baseball. Nor are most ordinary human virtues missing; you find in locker rooms the same mix of flaws and virtues that you'd find among most other groups of successful professionals.

So Tunch Ilkin stares blankly at his television set. Gerald Williams takes stock of himself in the harshest possible terms. Dwayne Woodruff considers whether or not he wants to return for another season like this. Chuck Noll, realizing the season is lost though not yet half over, considers what he can tell his team that will be credible. He tells me, "There are things to be learned in every game for some of these players. The ones who realize that will profit. There are opportunities for these players. Let's see who wants to take advantage of them."

Dan Rooney thinks about how this team's performance may have tainted the legacy of his father and whether to move those Super Bowl trophies. "Of course," he says, "you can't live in the past. But it's a past Pittsburgh is proud of, a past worth building a future on."

Mike Webster does not want to go out a loser, but there doesn't seem much he can do about it. Joe Greene remembers a season every bit as humiliating but doesn't know what conclusions to draw. Tony Dungy's patience has been pushed to the limit and beyond, but he refuses to change his manner, refuses to panic. "Every situation," he points out, "no matter how bad, can be seen as a test of character. It's time to see who stands up and toughs this out."

Individually, collectively, and for those Stillers fans honorable enough to resist deserting this malformed team, the 1988 season will be remembered as a long, dark night of the soul.

Most of the fans had hung in with the team longer than the media people, many of whom were in competition to see who could be first to brand the Steelers "finished." And who is to say that those who quit on the Steelers after they lost six in a row, the last few games of which were pathetic, didn't have reasonable cause?

Frank Krupka, who told me at the beginning of the year that he came to Three Rivers just to see good football even if the Steelers lost, says of the streak, "You know the worst part about having abuse heaped on you? At a certain point, you don't even feel it anymore. I think the boys have reached that point. That's a depressing place to be at. Is it getting to me? You bet your ass—I don't like watching this week after week."

Two of the kids I've noticed hawking tickets before games are standing over a small fire in a garbage can after the Houston game. As I pass, I say, "They're sure not making it easy on you guys."

"Man, it doesn't even look like they're tryin' to win," one says.

"Oh, they're tryin'," the other says. "They're just trash. And trash just can't look like nothin' else."

When people place their faith in other people, in an institution, in a cause—and in Pittsburgh, rooting for the Stillers means all three—they expect repayment in kind. When it is not there, they begin to disassociate themselves, much like in the animal world, where the pack will shun a wounded, unhealthy, or deformed member. Although some humans observing this behavior might think it cruel, it is an instinctive response compatible with survival. What's lousy about it when it applies to people, is that one apparent betrayal becomes the justification for another far more real one, and trust and faith are further eroded. It's not unlike the downward spiral of the team itself.

Says Dave Ailes of the *Greensburg Tribune Review*, "I used to think it was impossible to write too much about the Steelers. Whatever you had, they would read. Now people are beginning to turn away." Fewer and fewer ticket holders are showing up for home games. Three Rivers holds fifty-nine thousand for football, and about that number showed for the Dallas opener. For Game Seven against Houston, there were seven thousand no-shows, and there would be twelve thousand the following week against Denver. For the last two home games, there would be seventeen thousand and twenty-three thousand no-shows, respectively.

Of the fans who do come to the stadium, some separate themselves from the team by booing and jeering—not many, but enough to be heard clearly. When a punt is got off without a block, it invokes a mock cheer. If a pass route is run properly and the ball is caught for a first down, more sarcastic approval. There is nothing that insults a professional athlete more than mockery, because it taunts and ridicules the thing that motivates him—his sense of pride. Mockery upsets the normal order of things in his universe, where he is the Chosen One, and the fans are, well, the fans.

I went into the stands during the second half of the Oilers game and was scared by the hostility a few beers seemingly activated. One guy, naked to the waist, his face painted half gold, half black, screamed, "Quitters! Goddamned quitters!" for the entire second half.

During a time-out, I managed to ask him why he hated his Stillers so much. "I don't make shit and got to watch my ass I don't get fired. Look at those guys. They make more in a game than I make in a year, an' they're heartless, gutless dogs."

Then why the gold and black on his face?

"Damn it, they're my team."

When the Steelers trot off the field at Three Rivers after the loss to Houston in mid-October, they are showered with insults and curses. A thug yells, "Hey, Aaron, you bum, you move like my mother, and she's got a double hernia." His pal yells, "And she's been dead a year and a half, too." An intellectual hollers, "Noll, hey, Noll, here's a flash right off the wire—Forward Pass Legalized!" Other rabble are spewing obscenities. It has been pretty warm on the field, so it's a great relief for players to pull off their helmets and begin to cool before they get to the runway. Most are too wise to expose themselves to projectiles and beer poured on their heads. Only a couple of guys—Mike Webster and Tunch Ilkin—have enough stature to dare to leave themselves uncovered as they pass below the madding crowd.

When the Steelers, at 1-6, are playing Denver, Paul Maguire, NBC's colorful color man, will dump a pretty good line on them while giving halftime scores on the national network show: "Will the lady who left her eleven kids at Three Rivers Stadium please pick up her children. They're beating the Steelers twenty-one to nothing at the half." Players can handle a joke like that from Maguire; he played with some pretty sorrowful Buffalo Bills teams himself.

It is the Flies, though, who most effectively isolate this poor football team. Hubbard of the *Press* leads his story of the Houston game as follows: "It is as if the Steelers are being coached by Charles Spencer Chaplin, not Charles Henry Noll. Every week is another audition for NFL Films' Bloopers and Boners." And later, describing the Steelers' inability to get eleven men on the field on two separate occasions and their seven offsides: "Wooo, wooo, wooo, Three Stooges."

There is lots of finger-pointing in the media—finding fault and blame assessing seem to be matters of extreme importance now. It is what human beings do best from a safe distance when expectations are not met, when things have begun to fall apart. By now everyone in the press box has a carefully worked-out theory to explain the failure. Charles Henry Noll is prominent in most of them.

Noll comes to his Monday press conference after Houston looking like hell. His face is puffy, his eyes bleary, his hair unkempt. Noll haters would be beside themselves with glee to see him looking like this.

He says, "I'm not going to vent my anger on anyone but me," and it looks as though he's been doing plenty of that in the hours since the game. "Shouting and screaming make good copy and you guys would like that, but it isn't going to win football games. Talking about the situation doesn't get the job done. If getting it wrong is necessary to eventually getting it right, well, we've done that part perfectly."

Usually after a game, Noll meets with his team in a closed locker room and lets the players know what's on his mind. Although he's been critical much of the season, he has rarely exploded at them because he doesn't want to break what's left of their spirit. Sometimes, though, as after the Houston game, he cannot mask his disgust. Later, he meets briefly with the Flies and shifts into his "protect my team" mode. Then he showers and sits around with some of the coaches while they share impressions of the game. He meets Marianne, his wife, in the lobby and makes his way through the pack of autograph hounds in the parking lot. Often they'll stop for dinner at a quiet restaurant on their way to their home in the classy suburb of Upper Saint Clair. Noll, who is something of a wine connoisseur, probably has the most pleasurable moment of his day when he sniffs the bouquet and puts a glass of fine Chardonnay to his lips.

One of Noll's strengths as a coach, granted even by some of his detractors, is his ability to hold a faltering team together, a skill he's been asked to employ frequently in recent years. "Chuck Noll doesn't lose his football teams" is usually the way it's put. That's what some of his defenders, when you can find them, are saying now. But this team is more than faltering. And it seems to my untrained eye that so many of these guys are uninspired, playing without hope. Maybe the team isn't lost, but there is so little of the all-important intensity on the football field that there seems no way for Noll to make this collection respectable from here on out.

The Steelers' "sunshine citizen" fans have bailed out. So have many of the Flies. It isn't possible to tell the degree to which most of the players have succumbed. Because playing hurt erodes the spirit as it wears on the body, it is not possible to tell the difference between a player giving up and one who just has nothing left. Fortunately, there is a core of players—such as Ilkin, Little, Woodson, Brister, and Webster—trying to keep the mass of their teammates in the game. The Steelers are trying gamely to hang in.

How bad can it get? No one knows for certain. The streak can conceivably run the course of the season. A 1-15 year. Privately, a few players admit the thought has crossed their minds. They've read in the papers about Noll's first year in Pittsburgh, Joe Greene's 1-13 torment; and baseball's Baltimore Orioles lost twenty-one games in a row in 1988 and became a laughingstock. The possibility leaves them weak. Usually a saving thought follows: "We got to win one sometime—it's the law of averages." Even as they think it, they know it's hollow logic and a bad sign—when you turn to the law of averages to bail you out, as every gambler knows, you're in serious trouble.

None of the players I talk with know the e. e. cummings poem titled "nobody loses all the time." The title is ironic, since some people do.

Because it is also human not to surrender, not everyone has turned on the Stillers. As the team's fortunes fell, the silent voices began to be heard. A woman caller on Cope's show was typical of the countersentiment that mounted as the Steelers became an object of anger and ridicule. She said: "Myron, I've never called a radio station

before, but I've been listening to everyone jumping on the band-
wagon saying Chuck Noll can't coach and the whole team stinks.
What I'm hearing is a mob mentality. Don't these people know the
least thing about fairness? Haven't they heard of loyalty? If we listen
to them and always look for the easy way out of every situation, we'll
lose whatever it is that makes us special. No, Myron, these are not
real fans; they're second-guessers and front-runners. If we listen to
them, we won't be Pittsburghers anymore. We'll be just like all those
fast cities that blow this way and that with every fad that comes and
goes."

From that point on in the show, the general tenor of calls echoed
that same basic sentiment. Similarly, in the letters section of both
papers' sports pages, a surprising number of people expressed at least
reserved support for Noll and the franchise.

In Pittsburgh there was still some love left for the Stillers.

10

WELCOME TO ROCK BOTTOM

The week before the Denver game, the "Noll Must Go" forces were in full battle cry. Some Flies buzzed with rumors of Noll's imminent resignation.

On his local TV show, Terry Bradshaw, sensing a kill, went right for the jugular. Bradshaw's basic tack: *Yes, Chuck Noll was a good coach once upon a time. When he had the players. But the game has passed him by.*

The other Louisiana quarterback was critical too. Bubby Brister picked this tense time to pop off in public. Frustrated because his injured finger was keeping him out longer than he anticipated (or believed was really necessary), Bubby let loose with some off-the-cuff comments about Noll at a football smoker. Later he said he was just drinking a little beer and trying to have fun with the fans by saying some outrageous things. It didn't concern Bubby at the time that a Fly was in the crowd with a tape recorder (Ron Musselman of the *Valley News Dispatch*).

Among Bubby's more inflammatory assessments was that Noll's offense was so unimaginative and predictable "we might as well punt on first down." He also said the Steelers talent was poorer than that of the teams they'd been playing. (That one must have pleased his already frustrated teammates no end.) This inferiority was due to poor drafting, Bubby thought, and that, too, could ultimately be laid at Noll's doorstep because he had veto power. Later, since he couldn't say he was misquoted, Bubby told off Musselman and then wouldn't respond to any of his questions in subsequent postgame locker-room interviews.

What most of Noll's critics were unaware of was that during the week's preparations for Denver, Noll had decided to shake things up. The coaches were preparing the team to do three things differently: first, to play with demonstrable enthusiasm, exactly as in college; second, to simplify all defensive assignments; and third, to put some gimmicks in the offensive game plan. They might lose again, but, damn it, it wouldn't be the same old way; they were going to put some fun back in their football lives.

Bouchette of the *Gazette* watched a few of the late-week practices and said, "Those were without a doubt the liveliest practices of the year—in a few years, maybe."

Tunch confirmed this. "I played across from Aaron all week, and his fuse was mighty short. We scuffled and shuffled a bit." Merril Hoge said, "What the heck is it about me that wants to make Delton change my features? Because that's what he wanted to do at practice on Friday."

Tired of getting kicked around by opponents, the players were chippy when they took the field; there was lots of extracurricular pushing, bumping, and angry words. A few short, cranky fights broke out. The coaching staff welcomed the irritability.

Joe Gordon liked the simplification of the defense. "We have to have set an NFL record in allowing third-and-long first-down pass completions. That's a prevent situation, and it means our people don't know what they're supposed to be doing out there. It's time to turn to the KISS theory."

The KISS theory, Joe?

"Yeah, *K*eep *I*t *S*imple, *S*tupid!"

The Steelers seem to have fallen into some—ah, what's that word again? Oh yes—good luck. John Elway, the Denver quarterback, won't play. He went down late in the game the previous week with a sprained knee. Of course Kosar didn't play when the Browns came into Three Rivers and that didn't make a bit of difference in the outcome. Kosar was the key to the Browns' offense. Elway is another matter: He *is* the Denver offense. Bubby's still out too, but the injury advantage goes to Pittsburgh.

If the Steelers are collectively waiting for the law of averages to hand them a ball game, they'll probably lose yet again. If they choose to go out and, with total willingness, give up their bodies for a victory, this one is theirs for the taking. But that requires clearing the mind and focusing on what must be done, and there is much confusion in the brain when you have lost so often.

One of the things desperation does is cause losers to look for signs. I found a bizarre one on my USAir flight from New York to Pittsburgh the morning of the game. I don't bet on football, yet my reading of events on the plane had me wanting to bet my second mortgage. There was no way the Denver Broncos were going to leave Pittsburgh, Pennsylvania, with a win. Here's how I knew.

The 8:29 A.M. flight had never been sold out before, or even more than half filled. On the morning of the Denver game, however, there were lots of passengers. As is habitual on USAir, a row of seats facing into the plane were reserved for last-minute arrivals, and on USAir, "last minute" has a way of stretching into another time zone. Still, the table seats were kept free—until one of the handsomest couples

I'd seen apart from the pages of *Town and Country* entered and were escorted to them by a stewardess.

Husband and wife were unquestionably patrician, a type I'd never seen on this airline before. She, fortyish, blond, beautifully coiffed and garbed, tossed her full-length mink carelessly over two empty seats. He, older, also blond, magnificently groomed, tanned, trim, and outdoorsy, sat on the aisle and read *Fortune*. His plaid sport jacket was so smart, I had a pang of envy.

I stared. I wasn't the only one. Why were these people going to Pittsburgh? They were certainly not from there. And on a Sunday morning? People like this did not fly anything but first class; however, USAir did not have a first class. At least they were seated where first class should have been. You could tell they were uncomfortable on our egalitarian flight but girded themselves to tolerate whatever fate threw at them for the next hour and twenty minutes.

He was facing me. I studied his features. I knew that face. And slowly I began to connect it with, of all things, football. Then I saw a large diamond-studded ring on his finger, a Super Bowl ring. Football . . . flying to Pittsburgh on a Sunday. I dug out a not-too-recent Denver Broncos media guide and flipped it to photos of the team's officials. There was the face. Pat Bowlen, owner of the Denver Broncos.

We still hadn't taken off, so I decided to wait until we were airborne before going over and introducing myself. I'd tell him a bit about my project and hope he'd give me an opponent owner's perspective on the plight of the Steelers. I'd also get a look at that jacket up close. Maybe I'd meet Mrs. Bowlen too.

I never got the chance. A string of latecomers entered the plane and filled all those front seats. First came two Hasidim, sweating profusely and carrying old cartons wrapped with frayed twine. They pushed in alongside the owner and his lady. Mink coat, purse, and briefcase had to be moved to make a place. Then two large black

men came aboard, swinging lots of small valises. They roared with
excessive gaiety and took the open seats on the other side. Bowlen
and his wife had their personal space violated, engulfed by huddled
masses.

Maybe now they understood the price you have to pay when you
spend that extra night in Manhattan to see *Phantom of the Opera*
or some other hit. This is what happens when you pass up the offer
of a corporate jet and say instead, "We'll fly commercial. Only a
little over an hour. How bad can it be?" Reading the expression on
Pat Bowlen's face—a mix of smelling human bodies and trying to
think good thoughts—I guessed it can be pretty bad indeed. Their
noblesse hadn't been required to *oblige* this much for a long time.

Then it hit me. After Pat Bowlen endured a trip like this, was
there any way his football team could conceivably win this game? Of
course not. No way. It runs in threes: sweaty Hasidim; hyperactive
black men; a loss to the Pittsburgh Steelers.

No, nothing good would come to Pat Bowlen this afternoon, not
after USAir Flight 649.

A small black-and-gold sign is unrolled in the upper deck. It reads
KNOLL . . . FOREVER.

When one football team is as active and intense as the Steelers
are on this day and the other is as listless as the Broncos, it is hard
to tell which mood has shaped the other more. It is not hard to tell
which team is going to win the football game, however.

The Steelers are aggressive and determined. On offense the line
punches holes that the backs run through crisply. They do as well
faking into the line and running sweeps. Rodney Carter and Merril
Hoge share 200 yards rushing. As intended, the defense keeps it
simple and very physical. They deliver some of the best hits of the
year, and awe returns to the press box. Pittsburgh forces five Denver
fumbles. Twice the victim is Tony Dorsett, the local Hopewell High
and Pitt star, who is finishing off a superb career.

There are trick plays. And they work. Louis Lipps carries 23 yards on a double handoff, end around. Carter, on a halfback option, completes a pass to Hoge. More incredibly, a few times the Steelers go to the line of scrimmage without a huddle; Noll has thrown the no-huddle in there for comic relief. Fun is winning! And the Steelers' victory is one-sided fun, 39–21. Gary Anderson, the field-goal kicker, is six for six, setting a team record. His success illustrates a team problem, though. His longest kick is from only 37 yards out, which means the Steelers are not getting the ball into the end zone from in close. Considering how good it feels to win one, this is a quibble.

It is getting dark as the Steelers come off the field. More players than usual have pulled off their helmets. On the P.A. system Louis Armstrong is singing "What a Wonderful World." Merril Hoge walks toward the runway; his head is thrown back and he's singing along, savoring the moment. Today is the day he has proven to himself he can play in the NFL.

In the locker room he talks about the week's preparations. "At the first meeting Chuck said, 'Everyone in this room needs to evaluate himself.' That included the coaching staff. You could see that the coaches made big changes in the game plan and the lineup, so you could tell they'd been doing some soul-searching. When we hit that practice field on Wednesday, we were a different football team."

Gerald Williams says, "I don't want to talk too much about it because it's a private thing. It won't matter if I don't show improvement out there. But I'm going to try even harder to rev it up on every single play."

Ilkin notes that players are talking among themselves about how to salvage at least some of the season and their pride: "When we started losing, everyone thought, 'We'll snap out of it next week.' Now it's more a sense that we're in this mess together and we'd better reach down deeper and come together. I see some good signs in practice—guys are letting out their frustrations. We're sick and tired of being pushed around, even by the guys we work against in practice."

While the Flies wait for Noll at the postgame conference, they're buzzing about the Pope's unorthodoxies—end arounds, halfback options! "My God," someone says, "it's only a matter of time before we see the shotgun." In an obvious passing down, every other coach in the NFL has used the shotgun formation, where the quarterback stands four or five yards behind the center and takes a direct snap. He is, then, ready immediately to look downfield and throw the football. Noll considers the shotgun a bad percentage play—"More can go wrong with it than can go right," he has said—and he refuses to use it. Or even to consider using it.

Under any conditions. Ever.

Do these new wrinkles we've seen today mean that the Pope may be in the process of reinterpreting sacred doctrine? And will shotgun dogma now be reconsidered as well?

Noll sits down and says, "At the beginning of the week, we had a depressed football team. We knew we had to do things differently." Eventually, the subject of the gimmick plays comes up. "Oh, those. I got those in the mail." And does he plan to use them again in the future? "I have to wait for my letter this week and see."

Bruce Keidan asks, "What if your secret correspondent writes and you open the letter and it says, 'Dear Chuck: Now, the shotgun'?"

Noll waits for the laughter to die. His eyes flicker. "I think he's smarter than that."

It is announced that the team—essentially the captains and the assistant coaches—have awarded the game ball to Noll. It is a gesture of support in hard times, but it is impossible to tell if it is a true indication of respect. It could as easily be a political choice or a sign of appreciation for Noll's attempts to defend his players. Probably it's a bit of all three.

The following day, when Noll meets the Flies for the Monday press conference, they want to know why the team played with such enthusiasm. He is asked, "If this rah-rah stuff you used last week works, do you plan to do more of it?"

"I may have to. You know, there's some research that says it produces chemicals in the brain. Really." He conveys the impression he's been leafing through the *New England Journal of Medicine*.

In citing the virtues of rah-rah, he seems to have forgotten a story Ray Mansfield, a center on Noll's first two Super Bowl teams, likes to tell. "Noll did not give pep talks as such. He believed we were professionals and would motivate ourselves in our own ways. Once at halftime this young player who had been with us three or four games started getting emotional, crying and giving an impassioned plea. Noll gave him that look of his and said, 'Shut the fuck up.'" I guess that was before Noll learned about those brain chemicals.

In the *Press*, Gene Collier explains the victory as nothing more than the carrying out of a league directive. He has a fictitious league official say, "The system cannot permit, cannot afford, for the Steelers to go 1-7. It'll mean four consecutive losses in Three Rivers Stadium, which has never happened, and that will indicate they are fully capable of going 1-15...." Something is funny, he claims, when "The Denver Broncos, featuring a defense that has limited opponents to barely 14 points a game in seven weeks, presents itself to a Steelers offense that has scored three touchdowns in the past three weeks" and gives up thirty-nine points. He concludes that league parity has mandated the victory, just so NFL types can say, "On any given day . . ."

There has been a rumor circulating for about a week that Terry Bradshaw is seriously ill. The story breaks after the Denver game. Bradshaw may have a malignant tumor near his heart, probably inoperable. He is going into the hospital for tests.

GAME DAY 9: SUNDAY, OCTOBER 30

Pittsburgh (2-6) at New York Jets (4-3-1)

I've been assured by none other than Joe Greene that improvement, or even maintenance, of good team play can never be assumed from week to week in the NFL. "Even the excellent teams in the league can't be sure how they're going to play. One reason they're excellent, though, is that they can usually crank it up a notch or two when they need it." Nevertheless, coaches try for a predictable level below which a team is not likely to fall.

It certainly seemed unlikely that the Steelers, having hit bottom, been forced to search their individual and collective souls, and learned that respectable performance required from them maximum, enthusiastic effort, would forget that lesson. If the secret was the release of brain chemicals—endorphins, my medical research revealed—all they had to do was release them every Sunday at 1 P.M. Since they'd already been shamed so often, how could they not play hard every week from here on out?

And they do outplay the Jets statistically, emotionally, and physically. There is even a tricky variation on one of the previous week's gimmicks: Brister, who is finally back, fakes the ball to Lipps on an end around; the Jets' secondary anticipates a Lipps run; Lipps continues on without the ball and throws a nice block on a linebacker while Bubby finds Carter in the corner of the end zone for a touchdown.

But the Steelers will go on to lose 24–20, another blatant giveaway.

Two plays signal what is still wrong. Leading by seven with three minutes left in the half, Brister completes a neat swing pass to Hoge near the right sideline. Hoge catches the ball, but his legs get all tangled up. He stumbles in the open field and, untouched, drops the ball as he falls. Robin Cole, the veteran linebacker the Steelers waived in training camp as part of the move to youth, recovers for the Jets on the Steelers' 25-yard line. The Jets take it in just before the half to tie; the point swing on that single play could have been as much as fourteen.

Late in the game, with the ball deep in their own territory and the game still up for grabs, the Steelers send out their punting team. One reason they beat Denver was they went the whole game without a blocked punt. Harry Newsome, the kicker, a man apparently too shy and sensitive to have to live so dangerously, has been the object of ferocious rushes week after week because four punts have already been blocked and the defensive rushers can smell raw meat. The blocks have been clean, usually with defenders pouring straight in on Newsome and getting the ball and him at the same time. Newsome is easily spooked these days, looking around cautiously even when boarding the team bus.

Blocked punt number five ties an NFL record for incompetence. Cornerback John Booty comes through untouched to block the punt and set up the touchdown that ices the win. Theoretically, a professional football team should be able to punt successfully every time if the snap to the kicker is crisp, because there is a blocker for every defensive rusher. That is, if each blocker checks a different individual. The Steelers have not been able to sort this out. On the latest screwup, Merril Hoge blocks the wrong man and lets Booty, his assigned opponent, stuff Newsome and the ball. Hoge is singing the blues after this game. There are tears in his eyes as he tries to explain things to the Flies.

Noll comes outside the locker room to meet the press. His calm is scary; it is emptiness in the face of utter frustration and defeat. He's got nothing left. *Resignation* is the word; resigning is the most logical alternative, if I read Noll's face rightly. The mental lapses this team is capable of can break a strong man. Yes, I have the overwhelming feeling Noll will announce his resignation during the week. Either that or Dan Rooney will ask him to leave. I honestly believe we've seen the last of Chuck Noll.

He says, "We had a lot of people who played well. That's the shame of the whole thing. My job is to try to eliminate the mental and physical mistakes that go on week after week. . . ." The strong implication is that he has not been meeting his obligations.

Back in the locker room, I ask Hardy Nickerson, the young line-backer, how it feels to play as well as he did today and still lose a football game. His face, especially his eyes, sort out a great many complex thoughts, but he checks them all. "I can't really say any-thing about that," he says sadly.

I ask Bubby, "You played well enough to win. You've got to have a lot of frustration and anger. Where will it all go?"

"I'll go home and kick my dawg."

Mike Prisuta, who writes for the *Beaver County Times*, with pen poised, says, "What kind of dog you got?"

"One with a beard," Bubby barks. Prisuta wears a beard.

Robin Cole hadn't appreciated being cut by the Steelers; in fact, before he left training camp he had some hard words with Jed Hughes, the linebacker coach. He relished starting against his old team and had a very big game: eight tackles, two sacks, and the recovery of Hoge's fumble. It was the first time the New York Jets had ever beaten the Pittsburgh Steelers. Revenge doesn't get much sweeter.

GAME DAY 10: SUNDAY, NOVEMBER 6

Pittsburgh (2-7) at Cincinnati (7-2)

Looking back, there seems to have been a pattern. (Maybe that's what "looking back" always gives you.) In the beginning of the year, some good tries—certainly the effort was there—some bitter losses, and the slide to poverty. Then the Denver win, followed by a hard loss to the Jets. If the spiral pattern holds, the Steelers are poised on the brink of another plummet. Free-fall is a 42–17 whipping by the Bengals.

The final score is an accurate reflection of what both teams really are this season. It is of no matter that they play in wind and rain and sleet. The Steelers are falling to new depths. Listen:

Ilkin: "This was the worst football game I've ever played. I completely broke down on protection once. I'm humiliated. I'm embarrassed. It's bad, man. The only good thing, I guess, is that I'm still employed, at least till tomorrow morning."

Woodson: "All we were doing was standing in each other's way, like totem poles. I thought we were ready to play, the way we were fighting in practice all week. And these guys just buried us."

Dungy: "Nobody felt *this* was even a possibility." (It is unclear if Tony's *this* is meant to describe the game or the whole season. When you think about it, they're really one and the same.)

Bubby: "The best thing around here now is to keep your mouth shut."

As Bubby had left the field after the game, Cincinnati quarterback Boomer Esiason sought him out. Shaking Bubby's hand, Boomer said, "I was on the other end of the stick last year. I know how it feels. It's important not to get down on coaches and teammates."

It is impossible not to. Entropy—the physical principle of deterioration—has taken over after so much losing. Noll reflects it in the locker room after the game. Of course he berates his team. They expect that; they stunk up Riverfront Stadium. They do not expect what Noll says next: "The way we played today, maybe we should all go out and get law degrees."

No one can miss the reference. It is aimed specifically at Dwayne Woodruff, who earlier in the week received word he'd passed the bar. He is a lawyer. Although Noll had more than once praised

Woodruff publicly for his drive and intelligence, and Woodruff had in no way short-changed the Steelers in the process, Woodruff had been handing out cigars all week and now has played a terrible game. The combination is too glaring for Noll to miss. Woodruff fully knows he has played badly in Cincinnati, but Noll's snide criticism is an obvious cheap shot. Woodruff isn't the only one who got caught out of position or made dumb choices.

The Flies sense an opening, but the normally cooperative Woodruff refuses to comment about what Chuck Noll did or did not say in the locker room. Some of Woodruff's buddies will.

Delton Hall says, "You can't point fingers at one person. The whole team lost today." Then, when he realizes the possible implications of what he's said, adds, "But I'm not saying Chuck is right or wrong."

Noll's supporters insist it was not an attack on Woodruff personally, but rather, a way of saying the team is distracted, not concentrating on their present profession. Unconsciously there must have been a well of resentment building in Noll, and it burst out in a barely veiled personal attack. All one can say for sure is that Chuck Noll has to really be feeling the pressure of losing.

Predictably, he will not comment on what some of the players reported he'd said other than to insist, "Whatever is said between me and my players is between me and my players."

Bouchette's sidebar on the episode is headed NOLL'S REMARK IS IN CONTEMPT OF STEELERS.

The pressure has finally gotten to Noll, whose ability to handle stress is a personal badge of honor.

The bus to the airport is dark. No one is looking at stats but Dan Edwards, the PR man, and a few of the Flies. Outside, snow is falling. Delton Hall, whose season has been a mix of pain and anguish, sprawls across a double seat, turned toward the aisle. The

a.

b.

a. LONG SEASON: Coach Chuck Noll absorbing another loss. *Courtesy of the Pittsburgh Steelers and Michael F. Fabus.*

b. SUPER: The four Vince Lombardi trophies, intimidating icons to future Steelers. *Courtesy of the Pittsburgh Steelers.*

a. TRADITION: The late Steelers owner Art Rooney with his son and successor, Dan. *Courtesy of the Pittsburgh Steelers.*

a.

b. OLD PRO: For coach "Mean" Joe Greene, it was a long way from the championship seasons. *Courtesy of the Pittsburgh Steelers and Bill Amatucci.*

b.

a. RARE CELEBRATION: An elated Brister rejoicing with teammates in the end zone after a touchdown. *Courtesy of the Pittsburgh Steelers.*

b. PLEASANT SURPRISE: As the season progressed, Bubby Brister matured into a first-rate quarterback. *Courtesy of the Pittsburgh Steelers and Bill Amatucci.*

a. UNANSWERED PRAYERS: Rookie Aaron Jones wasn't yet the big impact defensive player the Steelers hoped for. *Courtesy of the Pittsburgh Steelers and Michael F. Fabus.*

b. TRUE GRIT: Merril Hoge gave it all he had on every rush. *Courtesy of the Pittsburgh Steelers and Michael F. Fabus.*

a. DEDICATION: Veteran Tunch Ilkin tried to maintain a positive outlook despite playing on a losing team. *Courtesy of the Pittsburgh Steelers and Bill Amatucci.*

b. END OF THE LINE: Center Mike Webster (52) finally called it quits at the end of the 1988 season. *Courtesy of the Pittsburgh Steelers and Michael F. Fabus.*

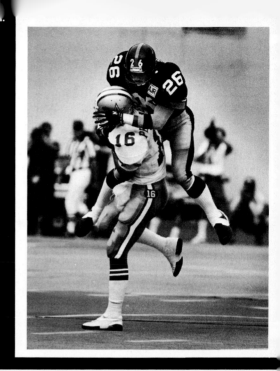

a. CORNERED BACK: Rod Woodson employing his hurdling skills in a flying tackle against Dallas. *Courtesy of the Pittsburgh Steelers and Michael F. Fabus.*

b. CLUBHOUSE LAWYER: Cornerback Dwayne Woodruff studied four years at night to become an attorney. *Courtesy of the Pittsburgh Steelers.*

a. TEACHING: Defensive coordinator Tony Dungy with Delton Hall on the practice field. Dungy left at the season's end. *Courtesy of the Pittsburgh Steelers and Michael F. Fabus.*

b. HOLDOUT: Star linebacker Mike Merriweather sat out the season rather than sign a new contract. *Courtesy of the Pittsburgh Steelers and Michael F. Fabus.*

c. LORD OF THE FLIES: Popular Steelers broadcaster and raconteur Myron Cope. *Courtesy of the Pittsburgh Steelers.*

b.

c.

a. PERFECTIONIST: Guard John Rienstra's pursuit of excellence led to ulcers. *Courtesy of the Pittsburgh Steelers.*

b. SPEEDSTER: Receiver Louis Lipps, one of the few Steelers stars. *Courtesy of the Pittsburgh Steelers.*

c. KICKED OFF: Harry Newsome [18] having another of his punts blocked, this time by the Browns. *Courtesy of the Pittsburgh Steelers.*

b.

c.

bill of his baseball cap is tugged down over his face, his collar pulled way up. He wants to disappear. He is holding the soft cast on his broken wrist upright, protecting it with his good hand. Last season, Hall, the All-Rookie, was an eagle. He believed he would always be an eagle. This season he is a gull. He appears to have hit his personal nadir at 4:45 P.M., November 6, 1988.

GAME DAY 11: SUNDAY, NOVEMBER 13

Philadelphia (5-5) at Pittsburgh (2-8)

"Ten bucks, great seats," is the hawkers' cry on the ramps. In the parking lots it's $8 for something decent. You can probably get tickets for $5 or $6 if you want to wait closer to game time. It would be well worth it to see Randall Cunningham, the Eagles' masterful young quarterback.

Cunningham seems to have no weaknesses—arm, athleticism, courage, intelligence, patience, youth (the order is alphabetical for convenience)—and will be worth seeing for years, but in Pittsburgh, even in these trying times, hardly anyone goes to Three Rivers just to see an opposing star, unless he played high school ball here. They still go to root for their Stillers, to look for a core of players, no matter how small, who will eventually bring back the good times.

Krupka's Blazer is not in its accustomed spot. I assume he, too, has joined the ranks of the no-shows. As I begin to walk to the ballpark, a voice calls my name. I turn. It is a younger, shorter, stouter Frank Krupka. His son, Frank junior, a man to whom I would talk about the Steelers a good deal in the months ahead. "My father told me what you looked like" is his introduction. "He's feeling a little under the weather."

We sit on lawn chairs on the asphalt, but it is not the same. Junior prefers Genesee, which we drink out of green bottles. He talks fast, quickly establishing his Aliquippa football credentials, and about the

old Stillers and what they meant to him and the men of his genera-
tion—standard male bonding stuff in Pittsburgh but no less important to him for that. He is talking about his life, so I listen.

Eventually I ask, "So what went wrong, Frank?"

"What? Nothing went wrong. It's the system that got to the
Stillers. Look at all the old great teams: Dallas, Miami, the Raiders.
You get penalized for being too successful; they make you draft low
and eventually it catches up with you. Unless you get lucky in the
draft, you can't get any real players. And lately the Stillers haven't
been lucky at all. You got to lose for a while in order to win. Crazy,
but that's the system."

"So the problem is the talent."

"Right. That and Chuck." He says what once would have been
unthinkable slowly and forcefully, implying, *And you can quote me
on that!* "People who think the only problem is the talent are nuts.
It's obviously something else when you look and see the team can't
even punt the football anymore. But people will say, 'How come
Chuck was a genius ten years ago and now he's suddenly stupid?' But
it could be. Not that Chuck's got stupid, just that he isn't the same
coach he used to be. It's like with a teacher. Once they know they
have their jobs for life, something just goes out of them."

Frank junior sprawls back in his chair, crosses his ankles, and folds
his hands behind his head, demonstrating a too-secure Chuck Noll
resting on his laurels. "They just lose that desire to be the best, the
edge to be great. It's not anything Chuck could help. He had his
time; his time is over." It's the Bradshaw scenario.

In parting, Krupka gives me his card—KRUP'S HOME IMPROVE-
MENT, INC.—in case I need more Stillers info. I don't have a card
to give him. If I did, I'm not sure I'd have offered it. The elder
Krupka, with his deeper love of football, as opposed to the son's love
of winning, is more my style.

*

Gary Anderson, who had been negotiating a new contract, signed a few days before the Eagles game. With a three-year deal for roughly $450,000 per year, he is now the team's second-highest-paid player after Earnest Jackson. It is not a good indication of the overall quality of your football team when the placekicker, good as he is, is the second-highest-paid player.

Almost as if to show he's worth it, Anderson kicks a 52-yarder to start the scoring. Bubby Brister, not Randall Cunningham, holds center stage for much of the game. Down by a point in the third quarter, Brister fades, scrambles, avoids Reggie White's rush, starts to run the ball, spots Louis Lipps open downfield, and launches the ball 60 yards in the air for an 89-yard, go-ahead touchdown. It is a breathtaking virtuoso performance, a franchise player's type of play. It's what Randall Cunningham usually does.

Cunningham's turn comes much later, almost too late. The Eagles trail 26–24 with less than two minutes left in the game. Cunningham launches a desperation throw long down the right sideline. Lupe Sanchez, in the game for Woodruff, who has sprained his shoulder, has a perfect angle on the ball for the Steelers. Certainly he can bat it away; there's a good chance he can intercept.

(At this point, you should be thinking, *Wait a minute. The Steelers might win this one. What could possibly go wrong now?* And you will have shown you know how the 1988 Steelers can kill you softly.) Sanchez slips on a wet spot and the pass is caught by Cris Carter for a 41-yard gain. Four plays later, an 18-yard Eagles field goal wins the game 27–26. It's spooky.

Bad as Tunch said he played at Cincinnati, that's how satisfied he is with his play today against Reggie White. "I've never been so nervous before a game. I'd heard how great the guy was and didn't want him to embarrass me. It's happened to me before. In the '83 playoffs against the Raiders, Lyle Alzado beat me for two and a half sacks on national television. I was thinking about that when I got ready for Reggie White.

"I can honestly say in my nine years in the league I've never seen a better pass rusher than Reggie White. And that includes all the games I've ever seen on TV. He's got it all. He's huge, he's quick and intense, and he's got every move, but what he tries to do most often is get you inside with his hands and lift you up. Once he's got you there, you're off balance and you're his. He's also a first-class gentleman, their player rep, too."

Tunch is ecstatic because he has kept a great player off Bubby on every play but one at the game's end. His reaction proves that a player can be on a team that's losing badly and still feel a sense of pride in having played well. His personal achievement has given him a charge. Still, he can't quite allow himself to seem too happy, so he slips quickly back into the team-man mode. "We should have won, I guess. It was a heartbreak when Lupe fell down. But that's probably just sour grapes on my part."

Theoretically, if every individual does his assignment well, the team will play winning football much of the time; that's the theory behind the 80-percent grading level. But this is a highly emotional team game in which the whole is supposed to transcend the individual parts. Merely doing personal assignments well neglects to take into account the crucial intangibles that make good teams better and give better teams a special aura, a unique character. Since the Steelers are not going anywhere as a team this season, players have begun to focus on personal achievement, a process known in the league as "playing for jobs." It's a motivation that's always there, but now it's become the *only* motivation for most of the players. And the coaches too. Individual survival is what it's about now.

GAME DAY 12: SUNDAY, NOVEMBER 20

Pittsburgh (2-9) at Cleveland (6-5)

Proximity and comparable talent once made this the best year-in, year-out rivalry in professional football. Cleveland is only 130 miles up the interstate. The Steelers always make the trip by bus. Fan allegiance is divided even after the motorcoach crosses the Ohio border, and the balance only clearly changes over to the Browns up around Youngstown. Hundreds of cars loaded with Stillers fans convoy the buses to the Ohio Turnpike. They show their colors—black and gold—wave insulting signs at Browns fans, and hoist beer cans. (Browns fans do the same thing when they roll down into Pittsburgh with their team.) And if the weather for the foray is not iron gray with driving sleet or snow, something isn't quite right.

On this trip the Steelers' caravan is spirited as usual, but smaller than usual too, made up of real hard-core loyalists and crazies only. The Steelers have not won in Cleveland since 1981. The driving snow is three quarters rain.

The Browns, having staggered through most of the season without Bernie Kosar and some key defensive players, are still in the chase for a wild card. This shows what depth and effort and leadership can surmount. Now Kosar is back, and the team's prospects are even brighter. Although Kosar will connect in the third quarter on a 77-yard touchdown pass, the Steelers will have already given the game away.

On the second play of the game, Brister, under pressure, is intercepted. The turnover becomes a Browns field goal. Then a snap clear over Harry Newsome's head—fear of another blocked punt has even gotten to Mike Webster—sets up a Cleveland touchdown from the 2. On the next possession, the fear proves founded: Newsome's punt is blocked and the ball run in for another touchdown. The sixth blocked punt of the season establishes an all-time NFL record for elemental incompetence. The game is 17–0 before the Steelers score their only touchdown. For the record, Brister gets sacked six times and the final is 27–7.

Looking down from the press box, Dan Rooney doesn't know if anger or shame is the appropriate response, but he's been coping with that dilemma all season. He tries to be in control when he says afterward, "Stupid plays took us out of the game. The whole punting situation is bad. I think it reflects our whole situation. At the end of the season, we have to evaluate everything we're doing."

It appears that events on the field have finally forced Rooney to acknowledge that Noll's critics may be right. The Rooney family has always been extremely grateful to Chuck Noll for leading them and the team out of the ruins of the NFL in the 1970s. But even gratitude has its limits.

There will definitely be changes. The only question now is how sweeping they will be.

"The thing that happens when you're losing as much as we are," explains Lupe Sanchez, "is that you don't wake up on Sunday morning thinking about winning a football game. You know you should be doing that, but you really can't. You wake up *hoping* you win, and as the day goes on, *hoping* you don't lose. And when you get out on the field, you're thinking more about *not* making the big mistake than *making* the big play."

The tests run on Terry Bradshaw show that the feared tumor near his heart is old scar tissue. He will be fine.

11

ARRESTED DEVELOPMENT

The Steelers' 1988 season had so far been like a disastrous traffic accident happening in slow motion. You see the destruction coming, but are unable to do a blessed thing to stop it as you watch the wreckage—a six-game losing streak and now four more—pile up. All in all, an extremely unpleasant experience for everyone involved, myself included.

When I first thought about doing a book about a year in the life of a professional football team and the city it represents, I chose Pittsburgh and the Steelers for a variety of reasons. I like the town and the people. I can't explain why completely: True affection can't be rationalized. But the town and its citizens invoked in me the Brooklyn of my youth, a place and a time I loved. Pittsburgh was very different, of course, but it was equivalent in all the ways that mattered—the texture and style of life in the old sections of the city and the towns up and down the river, the basic decency of the people, the Spirit of Place.

As a football fan, I admired the old Steelers. If football had an equivalent to Brooklyn's Dodgers, it was those Steelers teams. Doormats for decades, both teams eventually became the absolute best at what they did, but with a couple of important differences. The Steelers have stayed in Pittsburgh, even though the Rooneys have received windfall-profit offers from half a dozen cities to sell or move the franchise. Maybe someday the team will be tempted away from Steeltown, but it will happen only when the owner is no longer a Rooney, or is a Rooney in name but not in heart.

My original plan was to be on the inside when a team with potential to be a contender was put together and beginning to take shape. In other words, like Paul Zimmerman at *S.I.* and most of the other experts, I believed the '88 Steelers were going to be a good team, a likely wild-card playoff team, with even better prospects in the following years. It would be a success story. I could call it *The Steel Forge: The Making of a New Dynasty in Pittsburgh*. Everyone would then see how clever I was as a football prophet, and the world would beat a path to my book.

A long time before the Steelers sank to 2-10, matching Green Bay and Dallas for the league's worst record, one game behind Detroit and Tampa Bay, it had become unpleasantly clear to me that the success story I'd intended had flown. Even if the Steelers had won all the games that could've gone either way, I doubted I had a tale worth telling. But when the one-time unequaled Pittsburgh Steelers fell right through mediocrity to the league's wreckage, I realized I had a different, more offbeat story. I didn't particularly enjoy being the chronicler of other men's misfortune—felt a little guilty about it, in fact—but once it came full blown and I was there to document it, I had no choice but to tell it. At that point, like it or not, I became a Fly.

By the second Cleveland debacle, I had been witness not only to a second cycle of losing but to LOSING, writ large, on the psyches of the Steelers players, coaches, and team officials. It was LOSING as a constant presence in their daily lives, a force much stronger than the power of their resolve. It was breaking them in lots of little ways.

For one thing, they slouched more when they walked. When talking to Flies, they tended either to mumble with eyes on the floor or be snappish and challenge the premises of all questions. They joked about going around Pittsburgh in disguise, but it was not entirely a joke.

LOSING was its formal name, but it had many middle names: misjudgment, forgetfulness, inexperience, misunderstanding, fear, bad luck, miscommunication. There were so many ways to fail, so many introductions to LOSING and so few ways to do things properly, to grade out above 80 percent. Murphy's Law had kicked in weeks earlier. If things could possibly get screwed up, they would; someone would find a way, rarely the same person, rarely the same way. That was the killer.

"It's become endemic," Joe Gordon said.

"It's like a contagion," Tony Dungy said.

"Terminally ill" was Vic Ketchman's prognosis.

The deterioration of the punting game, as Dan Rooney pointed out, was an obvious symptom. Eleven men unable to sort out who is supposed to block whom indicates dreadful communication at least, and the distinct possibility that many of these players are not bright enough to play in the NFL. It's not unusual to find players who have the physical ability to play at a professional level but simply cannot master their increasingly complex assignments quickly, accurately, and consistently. Their talent enables them to hang on with a team for a year or two and then bounce around with other teams for a couple more. The Steelers seemed to have too many with this profile; that explains the need to adopt the KISS approach.

There were plenty of signs, other than the punting problems, that the 1988 Steelers were a team with a learning disability. There was a season-long tendency to take stupid penalties in the worst possible game situations. In and of itself, this was no great fault; you could interpret it as a sign of a pugnacious, overaggressive bunch of players.

Just channel those tendencies and you've got yourself a good rough crew. Make the aggressive mistake; hurt your team; get chewed out by the coach; don't make the same mistake again—that's the normal pattern.

But not quite the pattern with this group. Three games were lost because the Steelers sustained opponents' drives on penalties that handed them first downs. That can happen with good teams, though not exactly the way—or as often as—it happened on the Steelers. And on good teams, it rarely costs ball games.

One defensive series in the game against Houston speaks volumes. The Oilers led 25–7 in the third period. They had the ball on the Steelers' 49. Then, offside—Gerald Williams, 5 yards. Two plays later, offside—Jerry Reese, 5 yards. One play after that, offside— Aaron Jones, 5 yards. Then almost immediately, offside—Keith Gary, 5 yards. All the penalties came in obvious passing situations. Pulled downfield by the penalties, the Oilers scored again. The game was lost before the series of penalties, but they were an absurdity Three Rivers fans must jeer, for their *own* self-respect.

Down linemen want to get the quarterback. Desperately. In most of their contracts there are bonuses for quarterback sacks. The quarterback, in turn, teases them and tries to draw them offside with voice variations, but a lineman has been drilled repeatedly to keep a corner of his eye on the ball and not break until he sees it move. Aaron Jones is most vulnerable because he was signed as a pass rusher, and since the first game, against Dallas, he's been shut out. He's pressing for more but without any success. At season's end, Aaron will have 1.5 sacks, thereby missing his optimistic projection of 18 to 20 by a comical amount.

Aaron's particular offside in the Houston game was telling. He was offside even before he moved, having taken his stance with his hand already past the line of scrimmage. It's the same sort of mental lapse as allowing a blocked punt or having too many men on the field.

Jones had done the same thing four games earlier. Even more frustrating than the repeated offense was Jones's amazing explanation: "I watch where the referee puts the ball. That's what I line up on when I put my hand down. But then the center moves the ball up just enough to make me offside. It's a trick."

Then, because he was also guilty of lots of conventional offsides too, Aaron became a self-conscious player and was taken, or rather took himself, out of his game. It was characteristic of this defensive line that when Aaron managed to stay onside, one of the other guys would jump. Such was the atmosphere that had been created. *Deteriorating. Endemic. Contagious. Terminal.*

NFL game preparation is so sharp that most teams have even determined which opposing players, if provoked, are likely to blow their cool. In this the Steelers have been potential victims, not victimizers. "Some guys are talkers," says Ilkin, who even in his ninth year in the league will occasionally lose it, but never completely. "They'll try and take you out of your game any way they can. Spitting in your face. Coming under your helmet with their hands and trying to get a piece of anything."

Tunch swears, "The Oilers have cheap shots and obscenities as part of their game plan. They thrive on it. You know from the opening kickoff to the final gun, you've got a day of that crap ahead of you. Not all, but lots of them are chattering about how they're gonna kick your ass, run their cleats up your chest, just endless garbage like that. But it never stops. They grab, they hold and pull, they try to take out your legs, get under your face guard. You just have to try to avoid being sucked in. It's hard, though; as the game wears on, you get more and more frustrated because it never stops. Eventually you reach the snapping point. When you do react, you'd better try to be sure the ref has seen all the action. If he sees the whole thing, it'll be offsetting penalties and that won't hurt. But they usually just see the retaliation; that's fifteen yards, a bad one, and their strategy has worked."

If the instigators are spotted, they risk a penalty for unsportsman-like behavior. That's why the real pros, the ones you have to admire even though you hate them for it, do it with words. Cris Dishman (Houston), Wilber Marshall (Washington), Ron Heller (Philadel-phia), Otis Wilson (Chicago) are some renowned ball busters and cheap-shot artists, but the list could run to dozens. These provoca-teurs are so good they'll even coax the referee to watch their victim just before he's ready to blow.

Frustration is what an all-star NFL ball buster thrives on, and on the Steelers there's been enough of it to keep the league's taunters in clover. Most of the time when a fight has broken out it's been Jones, Keith Gary, or Rod Woodson for the Steelers. Since helmet and padding prevent anyone from getting hurt in a football fight (except the team that's penalized), it is pure symbolism.

Aaron Jones's raining punches on Philadelphia Eagles offensive tackle Ron Heller's helmet and shoulder pads did as much to lose that particular football game as Lupe Sanchez's fateful slip. In the second quarter, trailing by six points, Randall Cunningham was sacked on a third-down pass attempt. The Eagles should have had to punt. But no. After the whistle, Aaron wheeled and swung round-house punches at Ron Heller's football equipment. The referee observed the action from not five yards away. Heller, who actually hit Aaron from the rear before the ref was in position to notice, made himself look pathetic, cowering before Aaron's harmless bombard-ment. Flag. Personal foul, number 97. First down Eagles, who used the gift certificate to get themselves a touchdown. Remember, that was a one-point ball game.

Heller, a 290-pound Eddie Haskell type, takes pleasure in being a truly "offensive" tackle. After the game, he milked the incident: "They'll say I'm cheap or something. It's true I was laughing at them during the game, but the truth is they were more worried about what went on between plays. It was real junior-high-school stuff. When I saw that, I knew we would win. I think maybe they were trying to make up for a lack of talent."

Sure, Ron Heller was in Aaron's face all day, and, yes, he did push him from behind on the pass rush; still, Aaron knew how he was supposed to react. "I know I got to turn my back and walk away, but you see his face—he's laughing and taunting. It's real hard not to react. I've been taking stuff from guys like him all year. I think because I'm a rookie, they're picking on me. But I didn't understand why I'm the only rookie they're picking on."

Joe Greene has told him. Chuck Noll has told him. Some of the veterans have told him. Now I'll tell him: *They pick on you, Aaron, because you fall for it. They'll stop when you don't fall for it anymore.* If and when that ever happens, Aaron Jones might begin to become a professional football player.

After the game, Noll gave Heller credit. Grudgingly. "He's very smart. He saw a way to bait an opponent and it worked." Since training camp Noll had noticed a tendency in certain of his players to be drawn into fights. At first he saw it as spunk. When it started to cost the Steelers, he reconsidered. After the Denver win, he was annoyed about the fighting and said, "We're too aggressive—or is it dumb aggression? Obviously our manhood is so fragile we can be provoked." There is such a crucial, delicate balance between controlled and uncontrolled rage; some players take a couple of years to discover it, and some never do. You lose either way, but a frustrated team is better than a flat one.

After Jones won the Heller fight and lost the game, Noll told the Flies, "Maybe as far as Aaron's concerned, a surgical procedure is required." It was a line that got a rise. Anatomically speaking, could he be a little more specific? someone asked. Noll said, "Well, it's like that story about the guy who wanted to be Polish." The place went up for grabs.

Afterward, I wanted to know the Polish joke's punch line, but none of the Flies I asked knew it. They laughed, they explained, at the combination of "Polish" and "Aaron" and Noll and the timing. Jim Kriek, who's Polish, vaguely remembered the joke. He said it had something to do with a man who wanted to be Polish needing brain surgery. Removal was the suggested procedure.

Aaron was an easy target, but he was certainly not the only Steeler who had been playing dumb football. Or coaching it. The Steelers had been caught rather frequently with the wrong number of men on the field or the wrong men for a specific situation. It became standard press-box procedure for the Flies to count black helmets with each "packaged" substitution.

Noll said, "It's the simplest thing in the world for players to know when they're supposed to be in the game, but they get involved with things on the sideline, listening to their coaches, and lose track. We'll cut that out." Dan Rooney saw things differently: Not having enough of the right players on the field was a clear symptom of mismanagement.

What made Rooney particularly unhappy, once expectations for a respectable season had flown, was the inattention to promising young players. "No question," he said at 2-10, "that we went into this year with the idea that we were going to go with our young people. And I think it was the right move. But we have to start developing these young players. We have to let them come on. We go to camp each year and think we have this great talent and then they start tailing off. When I say 'every year,' I'm talking recent years."

What is surprising about Rooney's observation is that if Noll has one undeniable attribute, it is his ability to teach football skills. While some call him Emperor or Pope or, more recently, Ayatollah, he sees himself above all as Teacher, and he likes to talk about those skills. "I would have been a math or science teacher if I hadn't become a football coach. The rewards of teaching or coaching are pretty much the same. It is the sense of discovery a student has when he masters something he couldn't do before. When you see the sheer delight he feels afterward, it's very satisfying. Not that he got it from me; he got it by himself with my help. When that ability to learn to do things happens to an entire team, it's what football's all about."

Noll knows it hasn't happened to this team, though it has happened to a few individuals. He expected this to be both a fairly successful season and a "discovery" year. He thought he had the students to pull it off. When training camp ended, he said, "I think we have a football team." He meant, *I think we have some talented, teachable players*. He will not explain to anyone outside the inner circle what he thinks went wrong. Noll knows there is some raw talent on the team that hasn't been developed sufficiently. In other words, some decent students haven't learned, and there must have been something wrong with the teachers, the curriculum, or both. Noll's loyalty to his coaches, however, would never let him single anyone out for blame.

Because the Steelers were reasonably competitive early in the season, it was only when the Cleveland Browns came into Three Rivers and beat up his football team in the fifth game of the season that whatever doubts Noll had crystalized. Immediately after the game he said, "When everyone was healthy and playing well, I thought this could be a pretty good football team." When, for whatever reasons, his football team came apart, Noll took the blame. These were his students, he chose them in training camp, and they weren't cutting it. The teacher really could be faulted.

Once I asked Noll how he went about assessing what he called a player's "mental and character makeup." He admitted there was no easy way to do it and said, "There are psychological and personality tests they give players coming out of college, but they're not reliable. People learn how to take them and give the answers they know the test is looking for. The only way to find out what players are made of is to live with them through a season. Only way to find out. And that's what we're doing now." Presumably, if they haven't broken Chuck Noll by season's end and he's still in the coaching business, he'll have learned something.

After the second Cincinnati game—best remembered for his blowing his cool in the locker room with the law-degree crack—Noll told the Flies, "We ought to donate our salaries to charity; that wasn't professional football." Many coaches would have said "they"; Noll said "we." The bond between him and his players, at least as he presented it to the public, was unbroken; Noll and his staff always stayed after school to offer extra help.

This is a matter of personal belief bordering on a pope's creed with Chuck Noll: He makes his commitment to a team and he keeps it no matter what. He may end up wasting his knowledge, talent, emotions, and energy on players who aren't worth it, but quitting on them is an unthinkable alternative. It is not in Chuck Noll's makeup. The players and his assistants believe that Noll will not sell them out. It is one of the main reasons he doesn't lose the respect of most of his players.

Chuck Noll is never happier than when he finds a talented student who can develop over the course of a season. Dermontti Dawson started to become such a player for Noll in 1988. Early in the season and later, coming off injured reserve before the Kansas City game, Dawson was a quick, appreciative study. "Even though Hal Hunter was my line coach, Coach Noll paid attention and gave me some good tips. I knew all the footwork, but Chuck told me a few things about how to use my hands for leverage, and it made a heck of a difference." Said Chuck of Dawson, "I haven't seen many players in all my years here who can explode off the ball any better than Dermontti." There weren't many players on the Steelers about whom Noll could be even mildly positive.

Noll's staff takes its lead from him. They're always teaching and talking about teaching. Although willing to take their share of the blame for a team that hadn't learned very much, Joe Greene and the almost professorial Tony Dungy couldn't avoid mentioning how some of their students had disappointed them. "A lot of things I try to teach just don't stick," Greene complained. "Why? I wish I knew—then I could do something about it. I think it's a question of personal depth." By personal depth, Greene means the capacity to become the intelligently aggressive players they must be.

"The most disturbing thing to me," Dungy said, "is that some of the guys are not learning quickly enough, and the self-inflicted wounds just continue Sunday after Sunday. No matter how you preach or threaten, you just can't make inroads. In that respect it's like being a parent to a teenager. There is a strong possibility some of these guys might never learn."

Dungy clarified the problem even further: "Everyone has the will to win, but the will to prepare to win is the important thing in this league. It's not talked about very much, but the good players are simply more ready to play than most of the other guys. The other thing is the maturity to make right decisions under pressure."

Proper preparation and good decision making. Both required a depth that is rare among most young people and rarer among the new breed of young football players. Said Greene, "I don't just want a bunch of brutes, although the right players will have some brute in them. I don't want a con man, although a little of that wouldn't hurt either. People with the physical talents of some of the guys we've got could do the job if they just had the desire to learn all the workable techniques of an NFL lineman. [They] got to pay the price to become the smartest, toughest players they can be."

I suggested to Joe that some players won't do that for fear they don't have what it takes, and they'd rather not face the fact. He responded, "The courage to do that is what personal depth is all about. Confronting yourself first is the hardest battle."

After their loss to the Bengals in Game Ten, sitting alongside Jim

Kriek in the bus to the Cincinnati airport, I asked what he, not the Bard, thought was wrong with this team. Kriek is a Steelers loyalist and very much a Noll man. "There's something that's been bothering me," he said. "It's not just how many games they're losing that bothers me. It's *how* they're losing. Those dumb mistakes over and over. And I've got to say I really don't see the effort you'd expect after someone's been kicked around. Yes, I know about all the injuries. But there's something else missing—character. A Chuck Noll team always has character. That's what really confuses me. Noll hasn't put his stamp on this team. You got to wonder if he's lost his touch."

Then Jim Kriek didn't say anything for a while. The words, when they came, were not easy: "You know, I hate to say it, but maybe the game really *has* passed him by." You'd have to know how much Kriek admired Noll to sense how difficult it was for him to say that.

In the wake of the Philadelphia loss, waiting to talk to Ilkin about the state of his union, I read an anecdote he had taped to his cubicle titled "A Union Man and His Dog." Four workers, an engineer, an accountant, a chemist, and a union man, brag about their dogs. The engineer's dog, T-Square, can fetch sheets of paper. Slide Rule, the accountant's dog, can divide up cookies. Measure, the chemist's dog, can weigh ounces of milk. "And what can your dog do?" they ask the union man. That's when Coffee Break eats the cookies, drinks the milk, craps on the paper, screws the other three dogs, claims he's injured his back in the process, and files for workmen's compensation.

Tunch arrived with Tanner, his three-year-old, who zipped all over the locker room inside his father's oversized helmet. I asked Tunch if the guys had been paying their dues. There were reports that players around the league were not anteing up. If it was true, it could mean the players' union had effectively been broken by the owners' decision in 1987 to carry on through the strike by using scabs.

"I won't lie—this union has a credibility problem with the players at this point. But that has as much to do with the apathy of the players as it does with the union. I was just as guilty of apathy myself before I understood the issues. Once I took the time to understand the issues, I smartened up real fast.

"Even now, in my ninth season, I haven't made enough money to live off comfortably when I retire. In fact, the only way you can be substantially independent financially as a professional football player is to be a first-round draft pick and get very solid financial advice. Because of the high player turnover now—around twenty-five percent every year—there's no security whatever. The owners are letting guys go earlier every year. I look around the league and I see fewer and fewer grizzled veterans than I used to." The turnover was higher than average on the Steelers: Eighteen veterans from the '87 team did not make the '88 roster.

Being an active union man when the owners have total power to hire or fire is itself an act of great courage. Solidarity in the face of such power is the only equalizer the players have, and that's been broken. Less than half the players had paid their dues by Week Twelve. Many were waiting to see if they'd have a collective bargaining agreement with the owners, an unlikely event since there was litigation pending. Also, the $2,000 dues was quite a nut to part with all at once, even though the Steelers got their salaries in hefty installments every two weeks on odd-game Mondays.

Although the Steelers have Mondays off, many players come in for treatment or therapy for injuries, and a few work out in the weight room. On payday Mondays even more players drop in. Before they leave the complex, all the players walk down the long hallway past Dan Rooney's suite to Joe Gordon's office to pick up their envelopes. A few who really need the day off wait until Tuesday to pick up their checks. A very few.

But the main problem the union was having, according to Tunch, was a general irresponsibility among many of the younger players. "Most of them won't bother to read the union contract and don't even know what their basic rights and benefits are. They'll come to me and ask what they should do about all sorts of things, and I'm more than willing to oblige, but they seem awfully helpless. I guess it's partially because they were such talented athletes at such an early age. Almost all their lives, especially from around high school on, they have things done for them all the time. Except for playing, a lot of guys just have people around to do things for them. It breeds irresponsibility. That's why it's such a shock for so many players when their careers end."

There was nothing new in what Tunch told me. It wasn't, however, until the Steelers' record fell to 2-10 that I began to make a connection between the arrested emotional development of so many of the younger players and their inability to learn, to eliminate errors, and to grow in a football sense. After all, the Steelers had been giving their inexperienced players more minutes than almost any other team in the league. In other words, I connected Tunch's "irresponsibility" with Greene's "lack of depth" and Dungy's "immature teenager."

There seems to be a new breed of player coming into the NFL, even more immature and irresponsible than those of the recent past. They have exploited and been exploited by a cynical system of intercollegiate athletics that rewards them excessively (and often fraudulently) for honing their athletic skills without encouraging them to develop as human beings. More than ever before, college athletes are isolated from the mainstream of university students. They live in athletic dorms; their class schedules are tailored to meet athletic requirements; they are treated—and allow themselves to be treated—not only as jocks first and foremost, but as jocks exclusively. They rarely get to experience the normal social exchanges that are as important to personal growth during the college years as academic development may be. These conditions have been around for years, but the lack of responsibility of the institutions and the players themselves have become particularly extreme and blatant in the last few years.

You couldn't accurately call this a period of arrested development. It's worse than that because in many cases development hasn't ever really begun in the first place. "Terminal adolescence" is a phrase sports sociologists have begun to use.

The waste of personal potential among these young men is substantial and borders on the tragic in some instances, but there is also, ironically, a football cost. When Dungy's "smart and tempered players making right decisions" and Joe Greene's "players with some personal depth" were required to perform well in crucial game situations, the Steelers came up short. The problem was more mental than physical, but when the mind falters at this level of play, the body is lost.

When college stars come to the NFL, it is not only the talent level that must be elevated; maturity and the decision-making capacity that comes with it must increase also. Many of the Steelers' young players have professional-level talent. Throughout the season, the problem had been inconsistency, instability, lack of discipline—in other words, immaturity. It had been a problem on most of the younger teams, but there weren't any teams younger than the Steelers in terms of key-position players.

All season long, Tony Dungy had agonized over his most exasperating student, Rod Woodson, the team's most able athlete and one of its least able individuals emotionally. "He's got so much talent," explained Dungy, "he can make mistakes and still recover. He can take that little peek into the backfield and still be able to close ground on a deep receiver. In college, he could relax; he knew he could always catch up. Here that's not always the case. He's not used to playing under discipline, not used to playing against the great players in the game—Eddie Brown, Mark Clayton." Dungy's frustration was not that Woodson would not be a fine player—his talent alone almost assures that—but that Woodson might not allow himself to become the player he could be. Woodson has the physical potential to be a great one, but Dungy doesn't believe physical talent, even as great as Woodson's, is enough.

Woodson said, "I won't deny I've made some mistakes early, but I've cut them down. There's just fine-tuning necessary now. You can make this game so technical and complicated, but basically it's one man against another. And I believe I'm the better man."

Bubby Brister, who figured—if you believed his playboy image and early track record—to have trouble becoming the model of mature stability a young team leader is supposed to be, made a surprising decision in 1988. His father came up to Pittsburgh from Monroe, Louisiana, to share his son's apartment for the duration of the season. It was an unusual, if not a unique, father-and-son situation for the NFL. It might appear that Bubby was not mature enough at twenty-six to handle his first year as a starting quarterback without his daddy's help. The exact opposite was the case: Bubby was wise enough to know that the demands and temptations he'd have might be too much for him to handle in this, his make-or-break season. Why not have some loyal and mature help around?

"I knew," said Brister, "I was going to have my hands full with playing and studying, with public appearances and commercial commitments, and all the outside stuff I'm expected to do. This was going to be *my* season; I didn't want to blow it with distractions. It was my father's idea. He said he could handle most of the non-football stuff and leave me free to take care of business. It's worked out damn well, I think. We might be doing the same thing next year too."

The preseason rap was that Bubby was an airhead who could not master the playbook, the variations of formation, and the complicated terminology. As the season went on Bubby called more and more of his own plays. Said Noll after the final game, "I prefer a quarterback to grow to the point where he's calling his own plays. It's a sign of independence and maturity. You can't have true leadership on the offensive unit without it. As the season wore on, I could see Bubby's judgment and confidence build to the point where I was comfortable with him calling the plays. I expect that process to continue." Except for two occasions when he blew his cool, once because his injured finger kept him out of the lineup, and once over what he perceived as a bad call in Game Fifteen at San Diego, Bubby stayed, or was held, to the fairly straight and relatively narrow.

"When I first got here from my little town in Texas, I was really rough around the edges," said Joe Greene one day about his early years in the big time. "But the culture I came from wasn't as messed up as it's gotten lately. These kids are different. They bring to football all the problems of the culture at large." That's why the business of professional football has gotten so complicated.

The biggest mess in the "messed up" culture is drugs. In the NFL last season there were twenty-five players suspended for substance abuse, some of them among the league's biggest stars, such as the Giants' Lawrence Taylor and the Bills' Bruce Smith. Stanley Wilson of the Bengals was suspended and eventually banned from football for drug use on the eve of the Super Bowl. The Falcons' David Croudip died after he took an overdose. He was not a star; his name and his death have been all but forgotten.

Drugs are so much in people's consciousness that there is almost no such thing as simple human error anymore. A player misses a couple of tackles, drops a ball he should have caught, and the rumors start. Drop two passes and someone in the press box might mime an exaggerated sniff. "I saw him in a bar with some guys I know are into drugs," one Fly might whisper to another walking to their cars in the parking lot, and the rumors start to migrate. Dan Marino was picked at the bottom of the first round of the '83 draft partly on the basis of such unfounded rumors.

The Steelers, for their part, stayed clean in '88. Noll was asked in a press conference if he took pride in that fact. He simply said, knowing that moral superiority has a way of undercutting the moralist in time, "Our sense of pride is going to come from winning."

But Greene's allusion to the ills of the culture wasn't limited to drugs. He was talking about all the cultural baggage most kids carry with them into the NFL. "A lot of it has to do with a lack of basic understanding of how to act or to treat people. Like I said, a lack of depth. So we try to teach them here. I'm not sure many of them will learn, but the workplace is where it has to happen for them, if it's going to happen at all. These kids just happen to work on a football field."

Bill Nunn was the managing editor of the *Pittsburgh Courier,* one of the country's leading newspapers aimed at the black community, when he signed on as a part-time Steelers scout in 1967. He left the *Courier* and went full-time with the Steelers in 1970, focusing his attention mainly on southern black colleges. He was equipped for the job; he has picked the annual black All-American college team for years.

Nunn's efforts uncovered some of the Steelers' finest players, L. C. Greenwood, Mel Blount, Donnie Shell, and John Stallworth, among the most successful. Nunn's connections at these schools gave the Steelers a scouting advantage it took the rest of the league years to catch up with. Now Nunn, in semiretirement, is back to scouting on a part-time basis again.

"In a lot of the small black schools," he said when I caught up with him one day, "players had and still have a genuine relationship with the coaching staff and with the school. You don't see that at many of the big white colleges today. It helped them as people and that translated to them as players too."

But he didn't buy the arrested-development theory. "These aren't kids. At twenty-three, they're men. It's just that they are very inexperienced as players. And that will take time. When the Steelers were bad in the old days, players had time to develop. Now expectations are so high, they don't have time to develop the way they should. And though older players or coaches like to be critical, it's because they've forgotten what they were like as rookies. Just show them film from their rookie years and they'll quiet down real fast."

Merril Hoge was one player who made excellent progress. He seemed to draw blanks every once in a while, especially on blocking assignments on the punting unit, so they got him out of there and let him concentrate on playing fullback, where he could feel comfortable and be successful. Caught up in the season's academic theme, Hoge said, "I know we're all kind of in school this season, but pretty soon the schooling has got to stop. I want my doctorate at the end of the year."

Doctorate was asking a bit much. An NFL B.A. seemed a more reasonable goal for Hoge. And present another to Dermontti Dawson, the quiet man, who came on after being on injured reserved much of the season. Dawson started the last four games of the season, and graded out well over 80 percent in each of them. Since he's also an accurate long snapper, he's adaptable enough to play center as well as guard. Noll knows Dawson is a good one, a throwback to the kind of educable player he's used to. "Dawson's a young man who just keeps making progress. I believe he has an outstanding future in this league," said Noll when asked to find a bright spot amidst the gloom.

The Steelers had drafted center Chuck Lanza from Notre Dame

with the intention of using him to replace Mike Webster, expected to make this fifteenth season his last. It was assumed that Lanza would be worked into games as the season wore on, but most of the coaches didn't think he'd progressed enough to take the ball away from Webster. Lanza handled so few snaps there was no way to evaluate his NFL potential. If Lanza can't cut it, there's solace in the fact that Dawson can. Injuries allowing, wherever he plays, Dermontti Dawson should be in Pittsburgh a good long while.

Joe Gordon wanted to talk. You could tell because he'd pop out of his office and badger the Flies hanging around drinking coffee. The topics of conversation were usually former players, coaches, and Flies, those who had departed Pittsburgh in all kinds of ways and for all kinds of reasons. And the tenor was *If you think these guys are obnoxious, unruly, or difficult to get along with, you should have seen the guys in the old days*.

When it was time for Joe to go back to work, he said to me, "Everyone thinks it's still the football season. It isn't. It's the cerebral season. Everyone's got a theory about what went wrong."

I told him I had one too. He invited me in to tell it. He even took a respectful pose while listening, though he knew in advance that what I had to say would probably be off target. I gave him my basic arrested-development theory: The Steelers had the bad luck of going for America's youth at roughly the same time America's youth had gone to hell. This excellent teaching staff was instructing students with serious learning disabilities. By the time the staff realized this, the season had slipped away.

Joe Gordon heard me out politely. "Funny you mention that," he said. "Chuck recently said we ought to have more of a check into the backgrounds of some of the people we're thinking of drafting. Like a character check. But I've got to tell you, I've been here for a long time and have seen some real duds come along, guys you'd never think would amount to anything. And they were completely transformed. Why? Because there were guys on this team—leaders—who taught them how they had to behave on and off the field."

Gordon came to the Steelers as their PR man from the Pittsburgh Penguins hockey team in 1969, that woeful year the great Steelers teams were being incubated. "I took the Steelers' offer three months after Noll became the coach. We all grew up with the franchise. We were all in our mid-thirties. Chuck was thirty-seven; so was Dan Rooney. It was exciting stuff. I've watched Chuck over the years. If there's one thing I could say absolutely about the man it's that he has never lost a football team. I don't know how he does it, but I've seen some bad times and his teams don't quit on him."

I ran into Ahiro Okawa at the Pittsburgh airport after the Steelers fell to 2-10. I asked him if he had been following the Steelers. He rolled his eyes and smiled. He had. And the problem? "Not enough intelligent effort. Not enough quality control. Not enough Japanese players. Har-har-har."

12

THE GOLDEN 1:10

GAME DAY 13: SUNDAY, NOVEMBER 27

Kansas City (3-8-1) at Pittsburgh (2-10)

Some of the Flies dub the next few Steelers games the "Troy Aikman Bowl" in honor of the UCLA quarterback who will undoubtedly be the first player chosen in the 1989 draft. The team with the worst record gets first crack at him, and those Flies are rooting for the Steelers to keep losing. Strange system, this NFL draft; strange thing, this parity.

When I meet Frank Krupka, Sr., in the parking lot, he wants to know what I thought of his kid. "Fine boy. Really knows his football," I say. Krupka beams.

"But I'm always interested to hear what you've got to say, Frank."

"Well, I never thought I'd ever think this, but, you know, I hope the boys lose today. I'd like to see them get a first- or second-draft pick."

"The California quarterback?"

"Not to keep. Hell, I'm perfectly happy with Punky Brewster"—a fond variation of Bubby Brister. "There's a chance he could really turn into something. But to trade the quarterback to a team loaded with down linemen. Don't have to be a genius to see that's what this team needs. Throw Merriweather into a deal and we'll be up to our keesters in real players."

Something's wrong, I tell him, about a business where you've got to do so poorly to do well.

"I get the strong feeling," Krupka said, "these Steelers are like the lousy '69 and '70 teams. But we built to the championship through the draft. I feel the cycle's starting all over again, like I'm in that movie *Back to the Future*."

Even though it could conceivably bring him a better player in the draft next spring, strategic losing offends Chuck Noll. "If I ever thought about losing a football game, I'd have me put in jail," he says. There are still four games left, a quarter of the season, still time for the young players to improve and pass their final exam.

There are players fighting for jobs, and intense personal dramas at lots of positions. Brian Blankenship is a player on the cusp. A short (five feet eleven, 275) offensive guard, Blank signed as a free agent in '86 and was cut at the end of training camp after getting a good look in all preseason games. The '87 strike brought him back to the Steelers, who kept him on the roster until season's end. In '88 Brian was invited back to training camp and finally placed on waivers, but there was no interest around the league. The Steelers called him back after Rienstra broke his leg in Week Three. Blankenship has played as well as anyone expected in the games he has started, but he knows he's still marginal.

"You got to believe in yourself," he says, "and in the unknown. You never know what can happen, but you can always bet it will be something unexpected. So I'm always ready for the unexpected. Then, who knows, you get your chance and get the job done. So they look at you a little longer. Next thing you know, you're a player. They waived Tunch after his first training camp too, then there were injuries, they called him back, and now he's one of the best. So why not me?"

Brian Blankenship does his best on every snap. But many of the fans have begun to hope the team's best is not good enough. They'd like the Steelers to have the first pick in the draft, or at least one of the top three. In fact, it would suit them fine if the team tried less than its best and lost the rest of its games.

It's a ludicrous notion, the fan mentality at its worst. Surprisingly, some of the Flies subscribe to it as well. How exactly does a team go about ensuring a miserable record? How exactly do players who want to stay in the league go about trying to lose? Do the coaches put their worst players on the field in key situations? Noll will have none of it; he wants the Steelers to go all out to the wire. Besides, he argues, you can never tell how any drafted player, no matter how great a college star, will pan out as a pro. You've got to try to win to learn to win.

That's what they're doing against Kansas City. Grinding it out on the ground mostly, the Steelers lead the Chiefs 13–7 early in the third quarter when Harry Newsome runs out on the field for his first punt of the day. Naturally the Chiefs put on an all-out rush to rattle him. He gets it away—barely. The crowd gives him and the punting unit a standing ovation as they leave the field.

The game comes down to one last play with five seconds on the clock. The Steelers are ahead 16–10, the Chiefs have the ball 7 yards away from the Steelers' goal line, and there are no time-outs left. Steve DeBerg, the quarterback, has one play to get the ball into the end zone. If he does it, he wins; if he doesn't, he loses. In the wind-tunnel roar, David Little, the middle linebacker, screams to linemen in front of him and to linebackers on either side. The cornerbacks are poised on the balls of their feet, hands twitching, arms tucked out front for balance and to check receivers trying to brush past untouched a beat after the snap. The defensive linemen are down low and digging nervously with their rear feet, imagining they can get better traction off the Astroturf and a half-step advantage. The adrenaline is coming to a boil. These men will never be any more fully alive. They may not know it now, but it is an envious situation to be in, win or lose.

DeBerg wants his first-year wide receiver Kitrick Taylor, a great leaper, over the middle. Taylor cuts to the goalpost and for the barest fraction of a second he is open. DeBerg throws high for the crossbar. Taylor soars. The ball is three inches beyond his fingertips.

The Steelers' locker room is muted. In light of their miserable season, it feels unseemly to celebrate. Until Bubby gets there. "Goddammit," he shouts. "What's wrong with you people! We just won a football game. Hell, let's enjoy it." Slowly, and a little artificially, some energy does get activated. Game balls are presented to Brister, inside linebacker David Little, who has been just about the steadiest player all season, and fullback Merril Hoge, who has had another good all-around game.

Bubby holds forth afterward, describing his growth process this season. "I used to be hyper right before a game. I slept like a baby last night. I used to sit in here before a game nervous as hell. Now I know what I'm going to do and can be real relaxed about doing it."

Someone wants to know if Bubby feels he belongs up here, playing in the NFL. The question offends him. "Damn right I do, man." He also wants to mend an important fence. "And I want to say something about the people who talk about Chuck. Well, I think he's one of the best coaches has ever been." Since he's been one of the people who talked about Chuck, he must be chastising himself.

Across the room, Tunch is having trouble raising his left arm enough to roll on his deodorant. He doesn't want to offend, so he toughs it out, as he has been doing all season.

Charles Lockett, a second-year wide receiver, has started only his second game for the Steelers. In his first game, against Cleveland the previous week, he had three catches for 33 yards. Today he had four, for 60. His is an admirable story.

The coaching staff does not want to admit Lockett got his start because of a letter-writing campaign. That would be too unprofessional. But two weeks before the Browns game, a long letter appeared on the *Steelers Digest*'s letters page that took the Steelers to task for not using Lockett enough or very wisely. It ended, "Wake up Pittsburgh. Give Charles Lockett a chance to show what he can do."

The following week a more detailed criticism of the misuse of Charles Lockett appeared on that same page. Its chief complaint was that Lockett was being sent in almost exclusively on third-and-long passing situations. Put him in earlier, it urged; start him, in fact. Given the way the Steelers had been playing, what did they have to lose? Someone out there liked Charles Lockett. It wasn't until the fifth paragraph, which began, "As his father . . . ," that the reader realized who that someone was: Charles Lockett, Sr.

Later, the son said, "He wrote what he felt. I didn't know he wrote it until it was in there. My parents have always been supportive."

Most of the ribbing he suffered from teammates was good-natured. "Wonder if my daddy'll get me picked for the Pro Bowl," Steve Bono said just loud enough in the locker room.

Quite a season for fathers and sons on the Steelers. First Bubby's old man moved up to help him handle the pressures and responsibilities. Now Lockett senior was going to bat for his son in a very dicey situation.

Starting Lockett two games after the letters appeared was a classic Chuck Noll move.

GAME DAY 14: SUNDAY, DECEMBER 4

Pittsburgh (3-10) at Houston (9-4)

No one wants to use the word "revenge," even though that's precisely what it is. It tastes so refreshingly sweet on the lips it is almost worth the months of suffering. For a brief, satisfying, gloating moment. Almost.

Beating the obnoxious Oilers in a very physical manner in their own building, the "House of Pain," as Oilers' players had taken to calling the Astrodome, is good. Causing the Oilers worry about making the playoffs, which they thought they had locked away, is even better. Winning a road game for the first time all season, with everyone contributing, and doing it on a long, last-minute come-from-behind drive on national television, is the best. Payback.

I am standing on the sideline next to Vic Ketchman, watching the Steelers' four-point lead begin to disappear with less than two minutes left in the game. Houston has driven the length of the field to claim a win exactly as a superior home team is supposed to do it in the NFL, especially when the inferior team has played above itself all game long. Win it late and break their hearts is what the Oilers have in mind for the Steelers.

The Astrodome thunders and quakes beyond rational comprehension. I mean literally: The ground vibrations are so strong I honestly fear the House of Pain could crumble. If the last seconds against Kansas City were thrilling, this is shaping up as a horror show.

As the Oilers come up to the line of scrimmage 2 yards from the goal line and Warren Moon, the quarterback, flaps his arms for silence, time seems suspended. The huge arena quiets, but it is far from silent. At the sideline I can hear Moon shout his signals. On the snap, he steps back, hangs fire a moment, and breaks to his left along the line before he cuts diagonally inside, where he is tackled by two Steelers. Too late. The side judge's hands shoot upward. Moon has crossed the plane of the goal line. Touchdown: 34–31 Oilers!

The place quivers more precariously than ever. The assumption of the home crowd is that the home team has won, that they've clinched a playoff spot. The clock reads 1:30. I shout in Ketchman's ear, "Maybe they've scored too soon."

Amid celebration in the stands, the Steelers start from their own 20. The drive will have to be accomplished without benefit of signals; nothing can be heard. Nothing but a constant wash of sound. The crowd is the Oilers' twelfth man. The Dome-field advantage. I look into the stands; people are hugging, waving, twirling.

Every Steelers down is a timing play with players counting rhythmically in their heads on the snap. "We have a silent count," Webster would explain later. "Bubby just gooses me and we go." Players respond to the movement initiated at the hub and break into their assigned tasks. More things can go wrong than can go right. This is the Steelers' final exam, and it is being given *in extremis*.

Professional football at its best is a series of incredibly pressurized moments. Moving over trembling ground in a storm of roars, the defensive players transformed into dangerous, crazed projectiles, slicing in at fantastic, unpredictable angles (conditions that TV, for all its boom mikes and zoom cameras, cannot truly capture), the offense must stay juiced yet under control. Everyone must know the time and how many time-outs are left, where the sideline is, must avoid committing fouls and infractions.

This time, for some mysterious reason, the Steelers respond perfectly. The celebrants in the stands begin to pay attention as Pittsburgh starts to move surely through the chaos with excellent play calls by Brister, who mixes passes to his backs with key runs that keep the defense honest. Now the roar has purpose and is directed at the field, at the Steelers, trying to confuse them.

Brister stays cool, poised, and mature, as his team moves the ball confidently to the Oilers' 16. He finds Hoge open over the middle, and hits him. Hoge breaks tackles and runs into the end zone with the ball held like a torch high over his head. The sudden silence is stunning.

The line at the end of the stat sheet reads: "Steelers scoring drive—80 yards, 8 plays, 1:10." It doesn't say how much failed and wasted effort, how much humiliation, swallowed pride have gone into that drive. It doesn't say how many times this season drives not as difficult were botched and bungled.

Gary Anderson misses the extra point. He had made 202 in a row, the third longest streak in NFL history. Nevertheless, the Steelers win 37–34.

Ketchman asks Noll after the game, "Why do you think the team played so well when nothing was at stake?" Ketchman will claim afterward he knew he was waving a red flag.

Noll's nostrils flare just before he takes his run at Ketchman: "You guys keep saying nothing's at stake. You don't know football. . . ." (This gores Ketchman, who does indeed know football and prides himself on the fact.) "You don't understand professional football. You say there's nothing at stake, but you couldn't be further from the point. If they go out there and lay a dud, they couldn't hold their heads up. Pride is at stake. Those guys are trying to establish themselves. We've got a lot of young guys, and how they play and what their peers think of them is an important thing. What fans think, what *you guys* think is important. If they go out there and lay down, you think they can hold their heads high?"

Across the locker room, where he could not possibly have heard Noll's response, Merril Hoge says, "I'm not going to have to wear my baseball cap and sunglasses tomorrow. I'm gonna just go out there and let everybody see who I am." He might wave his diploma in their faces as well.

The Steelers had been insulted and kicked around by the Oilers six weeks before in front of their Three Rivers fans. If they had any character as a team, it was supposed to show itself right here, and it did. The Oilers were still their old chippy, obnoxious selves: "They were talking trash the way they always do," says Webster. "They tend to pick on certain guys they think might blow their cool or get taken out of their game."

This time, no go. As Noll puts it proudly, "They were physical *and* verbal. We just wanted to be physical. And we were." The difference in football philosophy between the Steelers and the Oilers—or more specifically between coaches Noll and Glanville—is shown in the awards presented to their respective special teams' players of the week. The Steelers' winner is given a basket of choice meats. The winning Oiler gets a combat helmet.

At his cubicle, Bubby is still acting as he did on the field, both hyper and controlled. "We kept together as a team. We kept the faith. And I can't imagine doing it under more adverse conditions. I finally think I've started to learn from some of the bad decisions I made earlier in the season." If that line gets into the papers, some of the teacher-coaches will read it with a hopeful smile.

Then, after quotes about the game have pretty much been exhausted, one of the Flies—in the name of no discernible justification—says to Brister, "You know you definitely blew your chances of getting Troy Aikman now."

Brister turns combative. Rightfully. "Maaaan, you guys pull that shit all the time. You've been saying all year, maybe Brister can't get the job done . . ." He wraps himself in a towel, moves toward the shower, turns, and hollers, "Do you still think that after the game you just saw!"

As the Astrodome fades from the rear window of the bus, something Noll said before the game echoes in my mind: "I think it's a terrible thing to call a stadium a House of Pain. It's such a privilege to be playing football in this league, they should have called it the Home of Joy."

Spoken like a man who is on a roll. The Steelers have won two in a row.

GAME DAY 15: SUNDAY, DECEMBER 11

Pittsburgh (4-10) at San Diego (4-10)

After the Houston game there seemed to be a more than reasonable chance for the Steelers to "win out"; that is, to win the rest of their games. First, they won that ugly, grind-it-out game against the Chiefs. Then the spectacular, final-drive victory as the world was coming to an end in the Astrodome. So why not blow out San Diego and then Miami in the home closer? That would make them only 6-10, but there would be momentum and a healthy seed already taking root for the 1989 training camp. And a bit of self-respect salvaged for the off-season.

Well, maybe not Miami on the final Sunday: Dan Marino would be coming home for the first time in five years and might decide to pick the Steelers' secondary apart. But surely these belatedly confident Steelers could beat the Chargers, a team with a coach certain to be fired shortly, loads of injuries, and Mark Malone quarterbacking against his former team.

On the plane there is an uncharacteristically boisterous game of liar's poker in the players' section competing with the normally loud Boo-Ray game in the rear. Fun probably *is* WINNING. On the football turf of San Diego's Jack Murphy Stadium, however, there is a logy lack of interest so palpable I believe I can reach out and touch it. I watch the entire game from the Steelers' bench; most of the players are slack-jawed and dull-eyed. It is very warm and humid in the Southern California haze.

Aaron Jones is hurt on the very first play of the game. "The pile just fell on me," he says after he is taken off the field. "I don't know how bad it is." He'll find out soon after the plane returns to Pittsburgh. It is no-football-till-next-year's-training-camp bad. It is arthroscopic-surgery bad.

As the first quarter ticks down, a voice in the quiet stands yells, crystal clear, "Somebody score." No one obliges until the second quarter, when Mark Malone hits Darren Flutie, Doug's bigger little brother, on a short scoring pass. Later in the same quarter Malone dives in for a 14–0 lead. I am supposed to be a dispassionate observer, but I can't believe the Steelers can be so flat. I want to yell, "What the hell's wrong with you people!" This has to be one of the most exasperating football teams extant.

Joe Greene on being flat: "I can't condone it, but I sure do understand it. When I was a player, there'd be games when I was flat like that—listless, lethargic. Football's a game of emotion. You only play once a week, and there's no excuse for being that way, but every once in a while, there it is. I used to try everything to get myself up: I'd insult myself, beg myself, anything. I'd tell myself it'll come when the situation called for it with the game on the line, but it didn't always. There's absolutely no accounting for it in certain games."

I had a theory about this one. Naturally. Just before the team left Pittsburgh, the *Post-Gazette* ran a story about salaries around the league. Somehow Ed Bouchette had gotten the figures from the NFL Players Association. There for all of Pittsburgh to see, next to each player's name, was his salary and alongside that the average salary for that position throughout the league. The Steelers, with an average base salary of $153,000 per man, were not just the lowest-paid team in professional football, but more than $100,000 lower than the league's big spenders, the Raiders, the Seahawks, and the Giants. The Raiders' owner, Al Davis, seemed to be getting the least return on his money; though his team would end the season at 7-9, he was paying an average base of $280,000.

Make all the jokes you want about how these guys were actually being overpaid, it is still a public embarrassment when, in a culture that measures worth by bucks, names appear linked to meager earnings. I believed it took the heart out of some of these proud men; at the very least it presented a major distraction just before a football game. This, I have to add, was a theory that got mocked roundly when I shared it with some Flies. I gave ground, but I believe it still because I imagined how I would have felt had my name been on the list.

Although the erratic Malone has played quite competently, it is Chargers running back Gary Anderson who wreaks havoc. He will end the day with 170 rushing yards, a personal best. What is so frustrating is that he runs the same play all afternoon, what Dungy describes as "a simple trap, a universal play in the NFL." What is more frustrating is that it is a Steelers bread-and-butter play, one the defense sees all week long in practice. Afterward Dungy will say, "Anderson ran it exceptionally well, but in our case different guys were doing things wrong all day, mistakes that made the play so effective." Mostly, they overrun the play and are out of position when Anderson cuts it back.

The Steelers act as though they can turn it on in the second half. Having come from behind the previous week, they just have to do it again. Who, but parents or a football coach, can know the heartbreaking effects of the teenaged mentality?

The Steelers do score on their first two possessions in the fourth quarter. The first is a touchdown pass from Bubby to Preston Gothard. If the name is unfamiliar to you, it's because the ball is unfamiliar to him. Gothard will have played most of the downs in every game for the Steelers in 1988, but have caught only twelve passes, just one for a touchdown. Gothard is the Noll prototypical tight end—he blocks. Later in the period, Brister runs it in to cut the Chargers' lead to three points, 17–14. The Steelers are no longer flat; neither are they truly enthusiastic. They hover in the lower range between.

This game turns on a referee's judgment call, a poor judgment, in my opinion. With possession once again and a chance to work the same magic he conjured in Houston, Bubby sets up a screen pass to Hoge. The defensive pressure on Brister is good and Hoge is covered. Brister wisely decides to throw the ball away, and heaves it accceptably high over Hoge's head. Referee Fred Silva tosses his flag— intentional grounding. Brister whips off his helmet and throws a foul-mouthed fit. Make that intentional grounding *and* unsportsmanlike conduct, leaving the Steelers with second down and 34 yards to go from their own 8. They are forced to punt. The Chargers, with field position created by the penalties, kick a field goal and win 20–14. So much for "winning out." So much for maturity and enthusiasm.

Brister's uncontrolled anger has killed an opportunity to win a football game. Yes, he's an emotional player, and, yes, it was a lousy call, but there is a higher level of professionalism called for here. No matter what, you never lose sight of the main objective, which is winning. The incredible lack of perspective and control throughout the season, which showed itself in dumb penalties and frustration fouls and fights, has reared up again. This time in a key player who is expected to lead. It's the next-to-last game of the season: Where's the growth? Where's the maturity? Exasperating.

Under the heading STEELERS CROSS THE LINE TOWARD STUPIDITY, Collier castigates Brister in the *Press* as one of those players who "virtually have no leash on their emotions and no concept whatsoever of even the general location of that thick line between necessary aggression and blatant stupidity." In light of how Bubby's behavior has affected the outcome, Collier's judgment is irrefutable. But it is also a patently odious call.

A word about the officiating in the NFL: *uneven.* Two words:

extremely uneven. This is tacitly understood by the league office, which assigns officiating crews on the basis of each matchup's significance. Games where standings will be affected, important TV games, traditional rivalries—these always get the sharper crews. So when Pittsburgh plays San Diego, the two teams with the worst records in the AFC, they don't get the best. The league office will never confirm the fact that there are priority assignments, but confirmation isn't needed. "Some of my best friends are NFL officials," says Cope, "but, let's face it, they were not all created equal. I've seen some meaningless games where some of the crew was assigned just because they live pretty close to the site." Having seen as many "low priority" Steelers games as I have in recent years, I'm disappointed with the quality of the officiating down at this end of the spectrum.

There can be no doubt that instant replay has made mediocre officials poor ones. Dozens of times over the course of the season, on a questionable out-of-bounds catch or a borderline fumble, officials have eyeballed one another for a moment, as though asking, "What did you see?" before making a call. The second-raters appear so afraid to be shown wrong by the camera, they start hedging their calls even before the fact. The call in San Diego was your standard NFL blown call.

Give me the guy who makes the definitive call every time—so what if the camera contradicts him from time to time? There are just not enough of those kinds of officials in the league these days, and the ones who are always work the biggest games of the day.

Preston Gothard is happy to have his annual TD, but like the rest of the Steelers, is bewildered by the empty tank in San Diego when it seemed likely the team could get its four in a row and a small measure of self-respect. He muses on the plane, "It's almost as though there's something in us that kicks in just when we're about to go forward a little and throws us into reverse." And what is that thing? "Maybe doubt."

A few days after the game Tunch Ilkin calls Mark Malone in San Diego. They had been close friends and hunting buddies when Malone was with the Steelers, and Tunch doesn't see any reason for that to change, especially since Malone built a home in Pittsburgh and spends his off-seasons there. On the phone, Ilkin can do a first-rate Southern California surfer: "Say, dude, can you give me a reading of wave heights in La Jolla?" Ilkin is calling to talk some football and to congratulate Malone on getting a game ball for helping to beat his old team. That, and to arrange their annual postseason hunting, beer-drinking, card-playing, male-bonding bash.

In retrospect the highlight of the San Diego trip was this Ernie "Fats" Holmes story Myron Cope told at the Flies' dinner before the game: "The Fat Man used to drink Courvoisier. I got back to the hotel real late one night—I should say one morning. The Fat Man was coming down on the elevator. He said, 'My-ron, you and me's going for a drink.' It was the last thing I wanted. So I said, 'Sure, Fat Man.' We're there at the bar when Phil Musick, a Pittsburgh guy, comes over and says, 'What're you doing here, Myron?' I say, 'The Fat Man asked me did I want to go down for a drink. If he'd have asked me did I want to go down to the bar for an enema, I'd take one.'"

The more I thought about it, that wasn't a Fats Holmes story after all. It was a Myron Cope story.

WHY SUNDAYS
WERE LOST

It became a major Pittsburgh pastime late in the season, this trying
to figure out why the Stillers failed. All the familiar theories cir-
culated. You heard them in the restaurant that features New York
corned beef on Liberty Avenue, in the Vesuvius pizza parlor on
Market Square. You heard them during intermissions of the Pittsburgh Symphony at Heinz Hall. You heard them at the Duquesne
Club. You heard them while waiting in line at the Mellon Bank. You
heard the men talking about them at the Ukrainian-American Citizens' Club in Carnegie while waiting for their wives to come out of
an Eastern Orthodox church.

You heard them in muffled tones at the Steelers' offices. Everywhere else, it was just babble. At 300 Stadium Circle, however, it
was important to talk it through and get it right. If the Steelers' brain
trust misjudged that one, they were dooming themselves to more
seasons like this one. Even if they analyzed the problem correctly,
that didn't guarantee they'd come up with the right solution for it.
Everyone knew something had to be done.

There was, I'd better add for accuracy, an interesting offbeat
belief held by an inconsequential minority, a minority of one, to be

perfectly honest. It was held only by Arthur McEnery, who had turned seventy-nine during the season. "Any season I live through I deem a great success."

McEnery also had a football justification for not seeing 1988 as a Steelers' failure. "This was a year the powers that be at the Stillers decided they were tired of just going along and playing average football. They decided finally to give the youth a chance, to reconstitute the team. Add a dash of bad luck, injuries, and the errors of inexperience and there is no doubt that many of the first eleven games were a disaster. That's the price you should expect to pay while learning. Nevertheless, if they win their final game this Sunday, they will have won three of their last five games from that point on. And they were so close in a few others. Although it took some time to find themselves, the latter part of the season was what any reasonable person should have expected."

But this is Pittsburgh. There are no reasonable persons where the Stillers are concerned. So much for perspective. Anything short of a Super Bowl is a failure to varying degrees. That mentality has just about ruined football here. And made me very glad I know Arthur McEnery.

In western Pennsylvania the 1988 Steelers' season was seen as the bleakest of failures. It's a shame the Steelers' organization wasn't able to steal a page from the Bush campaign, which cultivated no to low expectations and rode them to the presidency. It didn't matter what the organization said in trying to lower expectations; high expectations are part of football here. Recent Steelers teams, however, have begun to make inroads in that foolishness. They've helped draw the distinction between high expectations and false hopes. Things might become a little easier for future teams as a result.

The organization faced a difficult and delicate problem. It would have to do something fairly dramatic to retain its credibility, but it

also had to be able to see what there was of value in this team and
build on that. Dan Rooney did not seem like the sort of man to offer
up scapegoats or to make sweeping changes just to appease his
customers. He had the cushion of guaranteed sellouts for quite a few
more seasons, so he had some time to set things right. I had confidence that what he finally did would be based on what he honestly
believed had gone wrong and then finding the best way to fix it. The
worst possible course would be to overreact.

There were four major failure theories that emerged during the
"cerebral season." There were lots of individual variations, but it was
easy to lump them into general categories. In order of popularity, let
me call them the Weak-Talent Theory; the Poor-Coaching Theory;
the Parity Theory; and the Aberration Theory. (Then, of course,
there was my arrested-development hypothesis, but I'll spare you
that one again.)

Naturally, some of the four basic failure theories overlap—both
talent and coaching, for example, affect on-field performance and
even play off one another. But for the sake of clarity, it is wiser to
isolate one theory from another.

The Weak-Talent Theory

Usually expressed as "these guys stink," this theory was the most
widely held and straightforward explanation. It was impossible to
listen to Cope's sports call-in show in 1988 and not hear one phoner
out of two hit this same note. This collection of players simply wasn't
good enough to be competitive in the league, they argued, no matter
how much time you gave them to develop. That was not to say there
weren't a few athletes here with talent and some with genuine NFL
potential. It was to say that the overall level of ability just wouldn't
measure up to what a good football team should be, and never would
it produce an excellent team, certainly not a Super Bowl challenger.
Because the won-lost record had been so poor, this theory became

very difficult to repudiate, like a bad report card for a kid who tried his best.

But on closer examination the Weak-Talent Theory really doesn't tell you anything useful about a football team. In some rare instances you can spot a player who simply does not have the tools, the speed or the strength or the courage—demonstrable qualities all—and can be said not to have the "talent." Those types were effectively weeded out in training camp. The vast majority of the players on the Steelers, on *every* NFL team as a matter of fact, have the basic skills to be in the league. If they didn't, why would the Steelers' scouting and coaching staffs, men who have been so successful in spotting "talent" in the past, suddenly have lost their touch?

In other words, pure physical ability is only one component of a successful player, albeit a basic one, without which very little else can be expected, no matter how big the heart. With most of the players in the league it is almost impossible (great and obvious talents excepted) to isolate ability or "talent" from other qualities, the catch-all "intangibles" that make good professionals. It is true the Steelers didn't appear to have as many "feature" players as, say, the Redskins, the Oilers, or the Bengals, but a great many of those players weren't so obviously talented when they first came into the league; most of them weren't first-round draft picks.

Players will also tell you the difference between winning and losing is often a very thin line. Usually it involves attitude. Cincinnati Bengals 1987, 4-11; Cincinnati Bengals 1988, 12-4, AFC champ. Talent change? Hardly. And don't forget Tony Dungy's story of the difference between the two Steelers teams he played on, the '77 team that was good enough to win but didn't and the Super Bowl champion of the following year.

I could shoot all the holes I wanted into the Weak-Talent Theory, but still it is clear that the good teams have the better players and more of them. The '88 Steelers were a poor team. In a press conference during the first losing streak, a Fly asked Noll, "You've got seven 'replacement' players [bodies hired to play in 1987's strike games] on this team. What does that say about your team?" Noll said, "There are people who marry for a second time. What does that say about them? Maybe this team simply reflects American society."

Clever as his answer was, it didn't explain the fact that seven players who couldn't originally play in the NFL got back in because of the strike and made the Steelers the following year. Judging by callers on local sports-talk shows, there was a substantial number of Pittsburghers who believed Dan Rooney simply couldn't resist trying to do things on the cheap.

One of the things some pro teams do at the end of a season to check their talent against that of the competition is draft from their own roster. What's that? Yes, they take their rosters and draft from it exactly as though they were an expansion team looking for talent. They go about fifteen players deep, the core of a team's basic talent. Then they do the same thing with other teams and compare their core with the others.

On the plane back from San Diego, Vic Ketchman, Mike Prisuta, and I, having gotten into a discussion of the Steelers' nontalent level, decided to put the roster to the draft test. We drafted in order, each recording his picks on a separate list. Our basic football philosophies were quite different, but we knew we had to fill the skill positions while maintaining a nice mix of proven experience and young players with potential. Mostly, though, we focused on the pro-football definition of "talent."

After twelve rounds, the contents of our lists were remarkably similar, the only variation being the order of choices, and then not by much. By round fifteen, some slight differences of opinion entered because those last three rounds reflected more potential than proven ability. Overall, though, the lists held some respectable and promising football players. There were almost no down linemen—no surprise there; everyone knew that was a glaring need. Yes, Aaron Jones was on all three lists as a project still to be completed.

The core of a good young team was here. The problem was with the players in the next ten to twelve rounds. The falloff was especially noticeable when you compared Pittsburgh to the other teams in the AFC Central, Cincinnati, Houston, and Cleveland. It's on that second level of talent that the Weak-Talent Theory comes into play.

"You'll notice," said Ketchman, "very few of these players are impact players. That's where the Steelers need help desperately." An impact player is precisely what the term implies. He alters games; he leaves his mark on opponents and even on teammates. Everyone is aware of his presence when a game is on the line: on defense, opponents run plays away from him; on offense, he's the one who controls the football. The impact player is usually a star and a team leader, but not always. Ketchman was right: The Steelers didn't have any this season.

When at season's end, the Steelers listed the players on their thirty-seven-man protected roster, every player on our three lists was protected. It indicated that the guys who could play on this team were very easy to pick out.

The Poor-Coaching Theory

Bradshaw may not have fathered this theory but he certainly never disowned it in public. In the main it held that Chuck Noll had lost it. There were even a few extremists who went further, claiming he never had it in the first place, that he was just lucky; his players were so damned good in the seventies, they won four Super Bowls in spite of him. We can assume these looneys were out of tune.

The Poor-Coaching Theory centered on two points. The first was that Noll's philosophy of football was outmoded; hence, "the game has passed him by." These critics often cited his closed-mindedness about the shotgun, when every other team used it in long-yardage situations. Noll argued that it was a high-risk play, especially when crowd noise at hostile stadiums made the snap count impossible to hear. What's really involved, these critics contended, was an old fogey too stubborn to admit he was wrong after all these years.

The second part of this theory held that Noll personally had become too comfortable, too reputable; the drive and fire had gone out of him, and he just didn't hunger for success as desperately as he had when he was trying to make his reputation. There is no way to tell whether Noll has indeed lost his desire for success without being Chuck Noll himself. Not all teachers automatically succumb to the siren song of tenured security. Some do, some don't; it's an individual matter. I've noticed that among certain older teachers, if and when they do begin to decline toward the ends of their careers, a dormant sense of pride is reawakened in them; they find the fire once again and begin to teach like demons just to prove a point in the few years that are left to them, and they go out in a blaze of glory. Chuck Noll was humiliated by the 1988 season. Perhaps 1989 would be a "blaze of glory" season.

The argument that Noll's philosophy was outmoded had some legitimacy because his approach to the game was so damned elemental. Even though he tried the no-huddle offense a few times and employed some end arounds with variations and a few halfback option passes from midseason on, basically he refused to buy the trendy dazzle of offenses and defenses that come packaged in mysterious names. He'd seen all the trends in his thirty-five years in the league and made his decision. Noll's conscious choice to play football his way was not an intractable desire to prove a point, but a belief that football was not trends or technology but tough people, and would always be so. As Goose Goslin of KDKA radio once said about Noll, "Sure Chuck is stubborn, probably one of the stubbornest men

I've ever known, but he's not self-destructive. He can change when he sees a better way." Noll stayed with his system because he believed in it; it had worked and could work. He wouldn't be stampeded. He just needed more tough people.

The only way to know for sure if the game has passed Noll by is to see how a seasoned and reasonably talented and healthy team of his would perform over the course of a season. Lynn Swann firmly believes such a team would be very successful; Bradshaw is just as certain it would not. It is doubtful Noll will get many more chances to resolve the debate.

A slightly more sophisticated analysis of the Poor-Coaching Theory fingered the assistant coaches. The rough, hardworking, hard-talking, hard-drinking bunch of assistants of the seventies included men like Woody Widenhofer, who left to coach at Missouri, and George Perles, now head coach at Michigan State. Bud Carson, a brilliant defensive coordinator, went on to the Jets, and at the end of the '88 season was named head coach of the Cleveland Browns, the Steelers' arch rivals.

These coaches were replaced by younger, more temperate, softer men. The new fellows, the argument went, were too weak to be anything but yes-men to the strong-willed Noll. As a result, there was none of the old constructive friction that used to produce fresh approaches to things and a higher level of tension and energy on the coaching staff. Noll was never challenged, never made to justify decisions as he once was, never stimulated to experiment or to look for original solutions to problems.

There was no telling to what degree Dan Rooney subscribed to this part of the theory, but he became increasingly critical of the assistants toward season's end. He didn't think the young players were developing as they should. That was coaching. The protection for Harry Newsome was shockingly inept. That was coaching. The penalties, the mistakes, the lack of personal control all took the

Steelers out of ball games. That, too, ultimately was coaching. The Pittsburgh defense would finish last statistically in the NFL. Coaching. Rooney pledged a hard reevaluation of coaching in all areas and at all levels.

The Parity Theory

This one was a cousin to the Weak-Talent Theory, and like its relative was simple and complex at the same time. If you finish poorly often enough in the NFL, the draft offers you fine players. Theoretically, if you choose well, you can come up with impact players and good role players and be very competitive in three to five years. In other words, there's an incentive to do badly in order to do well.

The system appears to be working efficiently because many of the former "have-nots"—Philadelphia, New Orleans, Buffalo—have improved through the draft while traditional "haves"—Dallas, Pittsburgh, Miami, the Raiders—have become the new have-nots. If the system works perfectly, the distribution of talent throughout the league will become so balanced that both dynasties and doormats will disappear. It has already worked well enough to make Super Bowl repeaters as rare as impact players on the Steelers.

The draft has been around for a while, but in past years it was easier for the good organizations, especially those with excellent scouting departments, to maintain an edge. Bill Nunn, hitting black college campuses other teams overlooked, could find talent almost no one else knew about. For example, when the Steelers drafted John Stallworth of Alabama A&M in the fourth round of the 1974 draft, he had been hidden from the world. The Steelers convinced him to play in the defensive secondary in various college All-Star games so other scouts would not know he was really a great pass catcher.

But nowadays there are no more undiscovered talents. Says Nunn,

"We used to hold the draft right after the season. Those teams who knew what they were doing found the players and many of them became stars. Since they moved the draft back to late April, it gives some of the, shall I say, less effective organizations a chance to catch up." Which is precisely why the have-nots voted to push the draft back. "Now they hear all the names that are bandied about. You used to be rewarded for knowing your business, for doing your homework. Now a lot of the teams subscribe to big scouting networks; they get computerized stat sheets on every player in the galaxy. No, there aren't any more secrets in the NFL."

Chance, for better or worse, still plays a role in human affairs and can alter the best-laid plans. No one is more aware of this than the Steelers, whose painful memory of Gabe Rivera resurfaces every time they see an ineffective pass rush. Injury, contract or drug problems, the inability of a great college star to raise his game to the NFL level consistently—all these and more can undercut a high draft choice. Conversely, against all odds, a handful of lower picks may develop into players quickly and make a team a contender. But by and large, the draft system works to produce a bland uniformity.

The Steelers were penalized for playing above themselves in the early eighties. They did not plummet immediately when the dynasty ended and Bradshaw retired, so they did not have very many high picks throughout the decade. Usually they chose in the lower third of the draft. It is reasonable to argue, in fact, that Noll's excellent coaching kept his team competitive through the mid-1980s even without a quality quarterback; as a result, the team's talent level was indeed a cut below what it could have been had the Steelers excelled at being really lousy.

The '86 season was a case in point. As they would in '88, the Steelers lost six of their first seven games. But Noll held things together somehow and the team won five of the last nine. Insiders argue it was the high-water mark of Chuck Noll's coaching career.

Says Greene, "It was my first season as a coach, so I was sort of feeling my way. When we'd only won one game around midseason, I thought I was a jinx or something. I was also sure there was no way to get anything positive out of the year. But Chuck wouldn't let the team quit. His big campaign was 'See how good a football player you can become in the weeks that are left.' The young guys, especially, took him at his word. He just would not let the team self-destruct." But the Steelers hadn't failed badly enough to get better than the tenth player in the draft.

Have other teams given less than their best efforts at the end of a poor season to improve their draft positions? That's very hard to prove. It's also very likely.

The Aberration Theory

Don't let the fancy terminology, the diagramming of plays on TV, the computer-printout sheets used to analyze everything from offensive tendencies to players' muscle-to-fat ratios fool you. Football, even on this overorganized level, is a very inexact science.

In all human endeavors there is always a certain x factor—those unknown, unknowable, uncontrollable forces that conspire to undo the tactics and strategies of the most brilliant football minds. In our individual lives, we all know how we can be undone by forces beyond our control; yet we're unwilling to allow professionals the same leeway. We demand, since they're the experts making the big money, that they control the uncontrollable, solve the unsolvable. But that same x factor operates in their lives as in ours. According to the Aberration Theory, the Steelers were just having an x-factor year, a standard deviation.

Even though another one of Noll's strengths as a coach was his ability to make adjustments, on this thin team the resources simply were not there. There were games in the midst of both losing streaks when practically every man in a black-and-gold uniform was playing hurt or in an unfamiliar position. All the players could do was suck it up, do the best they could under the circumstances, try to improve individually and collectively, and stay the course.

Toward the end of the season, Tony Dungy was drawn as much to the Aberration Theory as any other. "There was, the more I analyze it, no way of anticipating this could have happened to us. I see it as an aberration, something that couldn't be predicted or controlled. I hope it becomes a very forgettable season real fast. Yet even with what happened you hope some things were learned after all, that it could be a stepping-stone to something better. I guess that proves I'm eternally hopeful."

But even the eternally hopeful Dungy had been chastened. His eyes widened when he realized something that was almost unthinkable. "What is really scary is that theoretically it can all happen again." Tony Dungy had looked into the heart of darkness; he would never again be the naïvely optimistic football coach he was before 1988.

To a man, the players refused to consider that such an aberration could happen again. Said Rod Woodson, "It was just a weird bunch of injuries and bad breaks, a million-to-one shot. You go through something like that once in your lifetime."

Just for the sake of argument, I said, "But there's nothing to stop those same injuries, the bad breaks, and holdouts from happening in the same or even a worse way, is there?"

"The world just can't be that unfair," he said uncertainly.

There was so much to fault in the 1988 Steelers, dozens of failure theories could easily be added to the main four. When you throw in Cope's observation that salary and career are such overriding considerations for players these days, or that the Steelers are the league's cheapskates, you end up with all sorts of possible recipes for failure.

For the Steelers, however, even in the midst of calamity, there were things to be proud of. Many teams would have fallen apart completely. There are lots of players and coaches who could not have resisted pointing fingers, giving excuses for their failures, publicly justifying themselves in all sorts of ways. Except for some minor pop-offs, there was surprisingly little dirty laundry aired in Pittsburgh. Given the perverse persistence of the Flies, there must not have been very much to dig up.

Tunch believed that, all in all, most of the players stood up to humiliation and disappointment fairly well. "When you're blown out of the playoffs early, there is a temptation to back off. It's so much easier to play this game when you've got the playoffs as a possibility. That's what's made this season so tough for me."

Frank Pollard, who was little used at running back, said, "It scares you that something like this can happen to a pretty good team. You know they're not gonna go next season with the same people. Sure, I worry, because I haven't gotten the chance to show what I can do."

If the players' futures were uncertain, it was much worse for the coaches, especially since Rooney had said individual coaching performances would be reevaluated at season's end. Bouchette of the *Gazette*, who seemed to be privy to more of what was happening behind closed doors than any other outsider, was quizzed by some of the coaches who felt in greatest jeopardy. "They wanted to know if I'd heard anything specifically about them," he confided. "A couple of guys were kind of scared. It felt weird for me to be in that position. I told them exactly what I'd heard, but it was never anything definite. I asked them why they didn't go to Chuck or Dan to find out where they stood. They said they didn't want to put ideas in anyone's head. I thought if they were that worried, they'd better start making some calls around the league. That's exactly what most of them were doing."

*

For the most part, at the end of the '88 season the Steelers avoided making a bad situation worse. At least they understood the difference between *losing* and *being losers*. Corny as it sounds in these cynical times, they salvaged a measure of dignity for themselves. There is something to be said for being able to avoid making a terrible situation a hateful one.

GAME DAY 16: SUNDAY, DECEMBER 18

Miami (6-9) at Pittsburgh (4-11)

It is appropriately gray and very cold in Pittsburgh. Snow has been predicted; it is only a matter of when. Young men are still hawking tickets on the ramps and in the lots. They'll take $3.

There are plenty of parking spaces for this one. It will be the smallest crowd of the year—36,051—but still impressive given the weather and the Steelers' season. The crowd is mostly in parkas rather than jerseys, but still in Stillers black and gold. They are cooking and drinking beer and tossing footballs, all with their breath vaporized around their heads. Fifteen Sundays have passed since I first met Frank Krupka. He is exactly as I saw him before that first game: in his Joe Greene jersey, straining a lawn chair, sipping an Iron City, patting my chair with his free hand.

"Welcome to the real Pittsburgh," he says. It's freezing, but Krupka has my beer, chilled; I have no choice. He wants to talk about loyalty. "You see how many people have been showing up in Dallas? Fifteen, twenty thousand. That tells you all you want to know. They're what I call corporation fans. You know, impress the customers, take 'em to a Cowboys game. Cowboys start losing big, so take 'em to a fancy restaurant instead. Our people don't pay in plastic. It's football they're here for, not because it's the place to be or to be seen. Even on a mean day like today. You got teams in this league that play indoors; the fans do the damn wave in the stands;

they even got cheerleaders. Can you imagine shit like that in Pittsburgh?"

In truth, I cannot. To answer would be a little insulting. I tell Frank that the Oilers, with their best season in a decade, have not sold out the Astrodome. When the Steelers played down there, ESPN had to buy up thousands of tickets in order to meet contract terms for televising the game. "You see," he trumpets, "a dome, the wave, cheerleaders."

Many have come out to pay their respects to Dan Marino, a good Central Catholic High and Pitt kid who remains a source of Pittsburgh pride. "How'd you like to see him playing up here?" I ask Krupka, repeating a preposterous rumor that had been circulating since Marino criticized the Miami quarterback coach, David Shula, Don's son.

"That's a tough one. Marino's the best there is and I love the kid. But you can't be sure how many good years we'd get out of him, and I've been getting kind of fond of the kid we have. He might have a future."

"Brister?"

"Sure, Brister. Why not?"

If I've heard right, here is someone who would stay with Brister over the best passer in football. Before I leave for the last time, we exchange addresses and telephone numbers. He asks me if I have his son's number. I say I do. The missus steps out from behind the Blazer, her face glowing. "This is for you, mister." I've almost forgotten Christmas, which is a week away. The paper is blue and green and the package is small and soft. I kiss her on both cheeks, European style. I want to shake Krupka's hand but he bear-hugs me first.

When I get to the press box, I scratch open the gift. Black-and-gold sleep socks the missus knitted herself.

Many of the Steelers live in Pittsburgh, and others plan to stay around for the off-season, working out at the stadium, following local amorous pursuits, trying to develop business connections. The fact that some twenty-five Steelers will have to face Pittsburghers until training camp begins next July is a not-so-subtle motivation in this final game. Miami, at 6-9, played a hard game the previous Monday night on national TV, and is a notorious warm-weather team, so the Steelers believe they should win. All week in practice, Noll has stressed how important it is to finish with a win to carry them through the off-season.

The Steelers' game plan is to try to run the ball, not only because Miami plays the run poorly and the weather makes passing tough— it's down to 23 degrees and gusty at game time—but because ball control will help keep the ball away from Marino much of the time. The plan works to perfection as the Steelers rush for over 300 yards. Under these malicious conditions, Marino throws two interceptions that are run back for touchdowns and throws no touchdowns himself. Those among the thirty-six thousand who have come out to see Marino are disappointed. But most are pleased by the 40–24 victory by their perplexing 1988 football team.

One of the most exciting plays of the game is a neat Louis Lipps touchdown on an end around. Noll has been using this play and variations of it ever since he told Keidan a mystery "correspondent" mailed it to him for the Denver game. Lipps has run, blocked, handed off, and even thrown a touchdown pass using this gimmick. He's also had a superb year receiving, going over a thousand yards for the first time since '85. He's been a pleasant rediscovery.

Late in the game Frank Pollard, a running back who has been injured much of the previous three years, gets in and runs the ball for just enough yards to move him into third place in career rushing for the Steelers. He has barely pushed ahead of his offensive backfield coach, Dick Hoak. Both are far behind Franco Harris and slightly in back of John Henry Johnson, a great runner and Hall of Famer of the early 1960s.

By winning, the Steelers demote themselves to the seventh pick in the first round of the '89 draft, still the highest they have selected since Bradshaw was number one in 1970. And by beating Dallas and Miami during the season, the Steelers have shown themselves to be the "best of the rest," with Noll beating two other great coaches the game has supposedly passed by, Landry and Shula. Is it a sign that he might be able to catch up to the game after all? Or was it debris beating rubbish?

If any further proof is needed that the Steelers were decimated by injury all season, only six players remained healthy enough to start all sixteen Sundays of the season. On the active forty-four-man roster at the end of the season, twenty-four players are either first- or second-year men. This was a very young, very inexperienced team.

Tunch is ebullient after the game. "Man, I love playing in the cold. I feel sharp, focused, really *alive*." The boys up from Miami didn't share Tunch's enthusiasm for frigid Pittsburgh; when they came off the field, their discomfort was painfully evident. "Me," Tunch says, "I feel I can do anything."

Tunch has survived another year in the NFL, playing almost every offensive down. And he's recently also found out he was voted to the AFC team in the Pro Bowl. He'll take his wife to the game, a nonviolent exercise that takes place in Hawaii in late January. It won't be cold enough for Tunch to enjoy himself, but what the hell, it's an unexpected Christmas present. More, because he was selected by opposing players and coaches, it is recognition by his peers that he is a very fine football player—a deserving one, in spite of the fact that Tunch is not totally convinced: "It's an honor, sure, but I'm not sure I'm a good lineman yet."

The game ball goes to Mike Webster, who has played his last

game as a Steeler, his 220th, a team record. It is Webster who usually gives out the game balls. "He's been," Tunch says, "the most dominant center ever to play the game, and you know what? He's only gotten one or two game balls over fifteen years. I just can't believe it."

Only a couple of guys will pack up and leave Pittsburgh immediately after the game. Most will come in Monday morning and say their formal good-byes to teammates, coaches, and officials. Even though there is little to celebrate besides physical survival—which of course cannot be underestimated—there will be a few small parties, though nothing too festive because almost everyone's future is uncertain. Insecurity has been a presence on this team from the first day of practice at Latrobe. It became more pronounced as the season unfolded. Still, they have endured. They have been to the depths together, and have shared something profound but something they'd just as soon forget.

There is a noticeable tenderness as the players who are leaving walk from cubicle to cubicle shaking hands, promising to stay in touch. They can't be sure they'll ever see one another again.

After the game Vic Ketchman and I walk to a restaurant for a sandwich and a beer. It has begun snowing fiercely. We sit and rehash the season. We've had the same conversation in fragments from midseason on; it has a life of its own.

Then we walk back through the empty parking lots of Three Rivers. The temperature has fallen into the low teens. Snow is driving into our faces. It is almost dark. Nevertheless, there is activity at the stadium's field entrance. A huge bulldozer, a steamroller, and other pieces of large machinery are coming off trucks and being moved through the entrance onto the field. "What are you guys doing?" I ask a guy with a clipboard.

"Ripping up the Astroturf."

I recall Joe Gordon mentioning earlier that there were plans to put down a new carpet, something with a deeper cushion, trimmer seams, and better traction. "You sure don't waste any time."

"Baseball season starts in a few months."

My rented car is the only one left in the distant parking lot. As I near it, I see an amber-colored bottle of Iron City standing up bravely on the asphalt against the howling winds. I approach it and try to tip it over with my toe. It doesn't fall. I kick it harder. Still it stands. It's frozen upright. There is a symbol of Pittsburgh here, but I'm not sure what it is.

14

DAN ROONEY DECIDES

Arthur McEnery lives in a beautifully refurbished row house just off Louisa Street not far from the Pittsburgh Playhouse and the University of Pittsburgh football stadium and campus. He has access to the library, so he is perfectly happy. The bookshelves of his second-floor apartment are crammed with the books educated people used to read.

While he is in the kitchen making us some tea, I pull a few at random. Every one has dog-eared pages and notes penciled in the margins. I ask him if there is any literary quote that illuminates the Steelers' season in some way. I assume he'll need some time to reflect.

Almost as though he's thought about it before—perhaps he was simply inspired—he says, "All happy families resemble one another; every unhappy family is unhappy in its own way."

"Tolstoy?"

"Uh-huh. The opening of *Anna Karenina*."

"How does it apply?"

"Well, even though everybody loves a winner, there's nothing really interesting about them. So the Forty-Niners win the Super

Bowl, and Bill Walsh goes out in style, but, really, what else is new? In human terms, as Tolstoy knew, the greatest tales are the tragic ones. And for so many of those young men on the Stillers, last season will be something etched in their minds. Let's hope it does some good. But even if they have a terrible season next year, it won't be the same terrible season. It will be a completely new unhappy experience. Unfortunately, while it would fascinate a novelist, it would just about destroy Chuck Noll."

This season came close to doing that. When I asked Noll after the final game if he thought this team would be improved in 1989, he did not glare a response. He did not sneer or look disgusted at me. He simply said, "We'd better be. I couldn't take another season like this one."

Without transition, McEnery says, with a revealing flash of eye, while he pours, "You know Pittsburgh has a new pope."

Since at the time Chuck Noll had intimated he might resign, I thought I could have missed an important announcement. "Has Noll quit, then?" (I had begun, in spite of myself, to mimic the singsong regional way of asking questions, almost like a Canadian. I did it again and immediately hated doing it.)

"No. We didn't replace the Pope. We've got two popes now. The way it was back in the fourteenth century when there were two popes, one in Rome and one in the Avignon. Except we've got 'em both in Pittsburgh." I'm confused. Arthur clarifies: "The new director of the Pittsburgh Symphony. Lorin Maazel. They've brought him to town, given him supreme power, and he's supposed to take the orchestra to the Super Bowl."

Maazel's hiring was not at all like Noll's arrival in 1969. The Pittsburgh Symphony has been one of the best in America for decades; the Steelers before Noll were one of the worst football teams. But according to McEnery, Maazel, like Noll, is a no-nonsense guy who has vowed to toughen up the orchestra until it is not merely one of the best but the absolute best. "I'd like to hear them both on Cope's show answering questions. You'd see they're both the same breed of cat, even though only one wears tails." Arthur McEnery loves his joke.

Even though he had pretty much made up his mind about what changes he intended to make right after the 27–7 debacle in Cleveland, when he said "we looked like Katzenjammer Kids out there," Dan Rooney had kept his counsel and his decision very much to himself.

It was a decision prompted by the kicking—or rather, the non-kicking—game. Weather conditions in Cleveland were dreadful for both teams, and the Browns blew a field-goal opportunity on a bobbled snap even as the Steelers were botching most components of their punting. After Cleveland had a poor snap and spot by the holder, the Browns' center, holder, and kicker ran over to the side-line and practiced. After their own mishaps, the Steelers slumped off the field and stood around looking embarrassed. Dan Rooney had been considering various post-season changes up to that point, and then he knew: The coaches weren't communicating the right attitudes and work habits, even about failure.

When the season ended, everyone in the Steelers' offices knew something was coming down, and quickly. Chuck Noll was in Dan Rooney's office for much of the week after the win over Miami. With the door closed. Rooney wanted three of Noll's coaches let go: Jed Hughes, the linebacker coach; Hal Hunter, who coached the offensive guards and centers; and Dennis Fitzgerald of special teams. Fitzgerald was no surprise; the punting failure had his name clearly on it. The others were a bit of surprise, especially Hughes, who had a particularly close relationship with Noll. Although the two men talked for hours, Rooney's decision was not negotiable. Noll could accept it or not. He considered resigning rather than firing men he believed in.

It was an agonizing Christmas for Noll, for Hughes and Hunter, for Rooney, who seemed ready to lose the savior coach who had brought football excellence to Pittsburgh and the accompanying renown and wealth to the Rooney family. It was an agonizing holiday also for the other coaches, because their futures depended on Noll's decision. They began to call friends on other teams looking for job leads. The Flies sensed some important changes were being considered at 300 Stadium Circle and swarmed through the fog of rumors that were spreading through the offices.

At one point, Joe Greene was so certain Noll had decided to leave the Steelers, he went into Rooney's office to thank Dan for all the good years he had spent with the organization as player and coach. Greene's farewell almost knocked Rooney off his seat, since Noll had not informed him of any final decision. For a moment Rooney thought Joe knew something he did not. Greene's gesture was, as it turned out, premature. In early January, realizing he wanted to continue coaching and that he wanted to do so in Pittsburgh, Chuck Noll reluctantly agreed to the three coaches' dismissal.

The chance to go out with a team on the upswing, if not actually in a blaze of coaching glory, was too tempting for Noll. Finally, it was stronger than his loyalty to his coaches; it humbled him a bit before the resolve and the ultimate power of the boss. He announced his decision to stay with finality: "I will remain with the Steelers for the rest of my football career." Significantly, the statement did not say "coaching career." Obviously, Rooney had to make it worth Noll's while to have him make such a pledge.

Although not on Rooney's hit list, Tony Dungy became the odd man out in the reshuffling. After Noll lost the battle to keep Jed Hughes, Dungy realized the man who replaced Hughes would be awarded the title defensive coordinator, since that was the only way to attract a person of the necessary stature and experience. Dungy would have to be willing to coach only the secondary, a demotion.

Dungy made some calls to friends around the league and discovered there were no coordinator jobs for him anywhere else; he would have to be satisfied being a secondary coach wherever he went. Insiders knew his defense at Pittsburgh had been broken by key injuries, huge doses of inexperience, and Merriweather's holdout, but how in the world could any team replace its own coordinator with a man whose defense ranked last in the league?

It was too much of an insult for Dungy to accept the Pittsburgh demotion. He had his choice of a few secondary jobs offered around the league and finally took the one at Kansas City. "I decided I'd rather work for Marty Schottenheimer [the new Kansas City head coach, who had quit the same position at Cleveland], who I respect a lot. The New York Giants made me an offer too, but I think my family will be happier in Kansas City. And I've got a great defensive backfield to work with. . . . I believe [it] is a team with good talent, a team on the rise."

I wondered if Tony was disappointed that Chuck had opted to stay on after first taking a high moral tone? Dungy said, "Chuck is a man who really believes in loyalty, but he was placed in a really difficult situation because he still wants to coach. At his age, it would have been hard moving on to a new town. He wants to see what he can do with this team. All things considered, I can understand why he did what he did."

Noll fared far better than Tom Landry did in Dallas. The Cowboys were sold to a group of investors headed by Jerry Jones for $146 million, and immediately Jones hired Miami University coach Jimmy Johnson, who had been a college roommate of his back in Arkansas. After twenty-nine years of service, Landry was out of his office in a matter of hours without so much as a "Y'all have a nice day now."

The Steelers played shop 'n' swap for a defensive coordinator. Rod Rust, an experienced and successful strategist, came over from Kansas City.

Around the league dozens of assistant coaches were fired after the 1988 season. Most caught on with other teams; quite a few did not. The NFL is as severe an employer for coaches on unsuccessful teams as it is for players.

A few weeks after the season ended, I ran into Ahiro Okawa at the Pittsburgh airport. I noticed his pale blue tie and couldn't help commenting on his new fashion statement. He said, "Different now. Last year, high-profile, always red tie, power, important, this man Okawa. This year, low-profile, blue, defensive coloring, like after-shave, cool, invisible. This man invisible. Har-har-har."

"If you really want to blend into the woodwork, maybe you shouldn't even wear a tie." I pointed to my open collar.

"Not correct to become so informal." Conversation about ties quickly gave way to his curiosity about my tale of the Steelers. "You know, in Japan no one would buy such a book." Oh? "No, no, not acceptable to write about a team that dishonors a city, dishonors its supporters, dishonors itself."

It bothered me that Okawa was making judgments from his narrow cultural point of view, the same sort of thing that Americans have done for so long. I explained, "My book will have nothing to do with dishonor. It's possible for a bunch of decent people to try their best and fail. When you make your best effort there can be no dishonor."

"Maybe that is the problem. People who worry so much about dishonor can go beyond what they think is 'best effort.' Maybe?"

I said, "Not everything in Japan succeeds, so how do you handle failure?"

His response surprised me because it was not sarcastic. "Yes, sometimes we fail, and that is when a most important decision is required. You must determine if the seeds of success exist in the failure. My favorite American expression: 'Not throw babies out with murky bathwater.' In Japan we say, 'Do not throw rings out with the rubble.' But idea is same. I like 'babies with bathwater' better. Is funny American image. See babies floating away, har-har-har."

Okawa was right. As tempting as it is to see the college draft as a panacea to a team's problems, the first thing the Steelers had to do was sift through the rubble of all those lost Sundays and try to find some gold rings. Or, in Okawa's terms, try to save some babies from the murky waters.

Murky as the season was, it was not hard to evaluate its most important discovery: Baby Bubby. Brister started the season as an inexperienced quarterback with only two NFL starts under his belt and ended as a key player most football people believed to be on the verge of a fine career.

Said Joe Gordon, "I'm not saying it was worth all the agony of the season, but the whole season might eventually be remembered for one thing—it was the year the Pittsburgh Steelers found themselves a quarterback."

Noll concurred: "Bubby really made strides last season. I was impressed with how he handled the adversity and never lost his enthusiasm. He can do just about anything you'd expect from a young quarterback, and he won the respect of his teammates. As far as his skills are concerned, there's almost nothing he won't be able to do eventually. I expect him to continue to improve."

Looking back on his season, Bubby drawled, "I was shooting for a higher completion rate"—his passing percentage was 47.3 percent—"and fewer interceptions"—there were fourteen in thirteen games—"but all things considered I'm fairly happy looking back at my first full season. I know I can play up here, and when I get really comfortable and things get automatic, I expect to play even better."

No, Bubby was not the model of consistency in the thirteen games he played, and no one considers him a proven quantity. But his

performance certainly indicated that, barring injury and other un-
foreseeable problems, Bubby Brister figures to be a fine NFL quarterback.

For most fans, the new football season begins with the April college
draft. But it is as much the final chapter to the previous season as
it is a new, clean page. It is not a hopeful time for some of the
veterans. Frankie Pollard, before he left for his home in Texas after
the final game of 1988, told me, "I used to like draft day. I'd see
who my new competition would be. It would get me pumped up.
I knew I could put the new kid away. Then, a few years ago, I started
to worry, but I used that worry to work harder. Now, there's almost
nothing you can do about holding on to your job, except play—if
they'll let you."

About two weeks before the 1989 draft, the Steelers declined to
offer Pollard a new contract. He'd played nine good years in the
league, almost triple the average length of service for a running back.
It was unlikely he'd be able to catch on with another team. Earnest
Jackson was let go too, a combination of ineffectiveness, attitude,
and a big salary. Steve Bono, the third-string quarterback, and Lupe
Sanchez, a reserve defensive back, were also released to make room
on the roster for the soon-to-be-drafted hopefuls.

The Steelers were very interested in Barry Sanders, the Heisman
Trophy winner and only a junior, who had been declared eligible for
the draft by Pete Rozelle. However, the Detroit Lions, who selected
third in the draft, were very likely to take Sanders, so there was really
no way to know who the Steelers' first choice would be. There were
so many holes to fill, it could have been any of half a dozen superb
college players, depending on who the six teams ahead of them left
available.

For weeks the Flies had been speculating in print about who the
Steelers would take. Troy Aikman had already been signed by the

Cowboys, and Tony Mandarich, the mobile monolith from Michigan State, would surely go second and Barry Sanders third. If the Steelers were lucky, the knowledgeable Flies agreed, one of the following players would be left there for them: Derrick Thomas, the Alabama linebacker; Deion Sanders, Florida State cornerback; Broderick Thomas, Nebraska linebacker/lineman; and Tim Worley, running back from Georgia. All of them were thought to be gilt-edged choices.

I asked Tom Donahoe, the newly named director of pro personnel and development, a young man moving upward quickly in the Steelers' tight inner circle, to evaluate some of the possible choices prior to the draft. "There are some great players down through seven or eight, then there's a big falloff, so we're lucky on that account. There's no telling which one will be there for us, but whoever it is will help us." He was saying, in other words, it was almost impossible to screw up this draft—on the first round, anyway.

Vic Ketchman had been high on Tim Worley all year. As the draft approached, he'd corner folks and, like a life-insurance salesman, try to prove how Worley was exactly the policy the Steelers' offense needed for future security. "He's the best back in the draft, period," Ketchman said. "He's big and he's fast. He can catch passes. He can block. And . . ." Here his eyes closed slightly and he smiled cruelly. "He is toughhhhhh."

All the scouts said the same thing. They called Worley a "feature" back, one who, like the old Dorsett, Dickerson, or Herschel Walker, was not a supplement but, rather, the basis of an offense. Worley is six feet two, 220, with great speed and excellent hands. Used in tandem with Hoge, the backfield could be estimable indeed in 1989. The threat it posed would give Brister many more options and make him much more difficult to defend.

There were some things I'd noticed about Worley that bothered me. He had been red-shirted his junior year, as the school reported, "to concentrate on academics." Then, after Georgia played its final game, Worley left campus, never returning to class. College was football; when football ended, so did college. Since I hadn't been able to shake off my arrested-development theory, I asked Donahoe, who had scouted Worley extensively, "How would you evaluate his character?"

"Well, he's not an altar boy, I can say that for sure, but he's not a criminal either. He's a smart kid who just didn't like school. Didn't like it when he was a kid. Didn't like it in college. But I have a good feeling about him."

"What's the family situation like?"

"It's actually pretty stable."

I assumed *stable* to mean he had a father and mother in the home.

Donahoe said, "No, no father. There's a strong grandmother, though." And I realized just how far out of shape the word *stable* could be stretched.

On Sunday, April 23, 1989, the fifty-fourth annual NFL draft ushered in the new football season. Out on the field of Three Rivers, the baseball Pirates were playing the Phillies and the crowd roar reverberated in the bowels of the building. This was where the Steelers were trying to build their future, block by block.

As usual, the Flies were given a conference room at the far end of the hallway, where they could write their stories, call their papers, talk draft, draft, draft, and still be near the spread of cold cuts, the salad, and the soup. The actual selections would be off limits to the Flies, in the players' meeting room near the other end of the complex. Tables there were set in a *T* shape. At the head table were the members of the brain trust—Dan Rooney, Chuck Noll, director of player personnel Dick Haley, and Tom Donahoe, and before them, the telephone with the open line to the Hyatt Hotel, where Bob McCartney, the Steelers' film director, who didn't mind going to New York to take a phone call and repeat a name, waited alongside an identifying Steelers helmet.

About thirty coaches, team officials, trainers, and clubhouse men filled the tables of the command post at Three Rivers. When it comes time to make the selections, the room is not always the most orderly place to operate from. This year Dan Rooney decided that right after Tampa Bay selected sixth, and it was clear which players were left, the brain trust would withdraw to a small side room and make the choice in silence. They would have fifteen minutes during the first round to let McCartney know who it would be.

ESPN once again carried the first day of the draft. Ironically, word of the Steelers' selections would not get to the Flies by coming fifty yards down the hall. Rather, Rooney would tell McCartney up in New York, McCartney would pass it to a messenger, who in turn would give it to Pete Rozelle. Rozelle would then step to the podium and say, "The Pittsburgh Steelers' first-round selection . . ." The Flies watching a TV monitor in the conference room would find out along with everyone else in the country.

Even as it was about to begin, the draft did not yet mark an end to the Steelers' 1988 misfortunes. The team had not exactly shopped Mike Merriweather around the league all season, though everyone knew he was available and all interested parties were welcome to inquire. However, as draft day approached, the Steelers, looking for a second pick in the first round, made a few calls to teams who were perhaps one good linebacker away from being a contender. Two days before the draft, the Steelers traded Merriweather to the Minnesota Vikings for their first-round selection, the twenty-fourth pick. Both teams were happy. The Steelers finally got something, a player, and just possibly a good one, for Merriweather. Jerry Burns, the Vikings' coach, said, "Now we've got the important piece we've been miss-ing."

In fact, as the draft was about to begin, neither team had any-thing. The Merriweather trade was contingent on his passing a physical exam and agreeing to Minnesota's terms. Merriweather passed the physical easily. The Vikings sent a team official to Califor-nia with five one-year contracts in his briefcase; if Merriweather signed one of them, there was a deal. Again Merriweather would not sign. Even as the draft began, Mike Merriweather refused to sign. It looked like even the Steelers' draft Sunday would be lost.

The early selections came quickly. Aikman—Dallas was announced five seconds after the draft began. Almost as quickly Mandarich—Green Bay, and Barry Sanders—Detroit. Then, with more deliberation, Derrick Thomas—Kansas City; Deion Sanders—Atlanta; Broderick Thomas—Tampa Bay. Deprived of all possible Sanderses and Thomases, the Steelers were up next.

As he said he would, Rooney took his three advisers into a quiet room. Since they'd had weeks to anticipate the predictable scenario that had just unfolded, they were ready. They wanted Worley. So why, as the story was relayed by insiders, did Dick Haley suggest before the final ticks of the fifteen-minute clock that maybe someone else, Andre Rison, a wide receiver from Michigan State, might suit the team's needs better? Instead of making their choice quickly and surely, there was this last-minute flutter. The Steelers took almost thirteen minutes to make the choice they had already agreed upon. Finally, Commissioner Rozelle stepped to the podium and said, "The Pittsburgh Steelers' first-round selection, running back Tim Worley of Georgia."

Even after the Steelers chose Worley, they did not know if Merriweather had agreed to Minnesota's terms. There had been a snag over a signing bonus; the amount, in the half-million-dollar range, was agreeable, but at issue was the method of payment. Merriweather insisted on a no-interest loan, for tax purposes, no doubt. Finally, word that Merriweather had signed came to the Flies after the tenth player had been selected. A mock cheer went up. The Steelers selected Tom Ricketts, a three-hundred-pound offensive tackle, a local kid from the University of Pittsburgh. The long Merriweather ordeal was over, and with it, the '88 season came to an end.

*

Almost. There remained the matter of what to do about the Super Bowl trophies. It had taken almost a season's worth of soul-searching, but Dan Rooney told me he had finally come to a decision. He smiled when he revealed it, like a man who has found wisdom after a painful struggle. "First," he said, "we're going to open up the lobby. A sign of a whole new era. Take out the wall and put in glass. It's too gloomy in here. Let the light in, let people on the outside look in and see what the Steelers are all about."

I asked, "And when they look at the center of the lobby, what will they see?"

"You mean the trophies. They'll see them. But not in the same way as before. We're going to separate them, not have all four in a clump. Those four trophies together like that were too much for some of the players to live up to. But they also gave the impression, clumped together, [that] they were a completed set. There was no room for another one under that glass. So we're going to spread them around the lobby. Two separated on each wall so they won't be too much to look at all at once. At the same time it will give the impression that there's plenty of space along the wall for another one or two in the years to come."

A perfect solution for an impossible dilemma. Hold on to the tradition but still try to take some of the stifling, overbearing weight away from it.

The remodeling of the lobby was supposed to begin in the summer. Until then the trophy case would remain an imposing sight for the dozens of players who came in every day for therapy, to work with the weights, to throw the ball around. Bouchette of the *Gazette* got word from a photographer that Bubby was taking some snaps from Dermontti Dawson and passing easily to loping receivers on the field before a baseball game. Nothing remarkable about that, except that Bubby was lining up four yards behind Dawson and taking long snaps. He was throwing from the shotgun.

In Pittsburgh any connection between Noll and the shotgun is big news, like Maazel conducting the *Eroica* Symphony from the balcony. Bouchette rushed out to the park and tried to get confirmation from Bubby that Noll was behind this experiment. Brister, who stayed crankily in his protective media pocket, said, "You'll have to talk to Coach." The fact that Dawson was the long snapper also suggested he'd replace Mike Webster at center.

Although Noll told Bouchette he was just examining various options for the next season, the shotgun was never before even a possibility. So the Pope was seriously considering making a former heresy part of the new litany for the 1989 congregation. Had he finally yielded to the critics' complaints of terminal fuddy-duddyism and unyielding arrogance? Never. He simply suggested with an enigmatic smile that there were more things in heaven and earth than we uninitiated could possibly contain in our philosophies.

When I left the Steelers' offices for the last time, the lobby reconstruction still hadn't begun. The trophies had not been broken up; they were, as usual, in a cluster of four encased in glass, beneath a spotlight. No one was around. I walked close. A typewriter clacked in the distance. I imagined Art Rooney was there again, his ruddy face and long cigar reflected in the glass. I realized that after a season of lost Sundays I really knew nothing more about why certain teams perform better than they should and others worse. Maybe, as Art Rooney suggested, luck is the crucial element. He had seen much of failure and astonishing success over a richly mottled lifetime.

That was the answer I was prepared to accept when I began to hear the names again, more subdued than ever before, a whispered catalog—Blount, Swann, Bradshaw, Harris, Greene, Lambert, Shell, Stallworth, Webster, Ham, Greenwood, Russell, Bleier, Gerela, White, Fuqua, Furness, Banaszak . . . Noll . . . the Chief.

In 1985, SAM TOPEROFF, author of six novels and a memoir, left two decades of comfort as a tenured university professor for life on the rugged frontier of free-lancing. His journalism and fiction have appeared in *The Atlantic, The New York Times Magazine, Reader's Digest,* and *Inside Sports,* among other publications. He is a frequent contributor to *Sports Illustrated*.

Mr. Toperoff lives in Huntington, Long Island, and Champ Clavel, France (where he spent thirteen summers building a chalet), with Faith Potter Toperoff, their daughter, Lily, and the incomparable poodle Ashley.

In Europe he has reported on French thoroughbred breeding and racing, the Soviet's greatest basketball player, the resurgence of the Marseille soccer team, the manic state of Italian basketball, a round of golf played in two countries, the world escargot-eating championships, and, most recently, the NFL-sponsored Worldwide American Football League (WAFL), which will begin play in four European cities in 1990.